teach
yourself®

dog training

dog training
association of
pet dog trainers

WARRINGTON BOROUGH COUNCIL	
H J	25/08/2005
636.7	£8.99

For over 60 years, more than 40 million people have learnt over 750 subjects the **teach yourself** way, with impressive results.

be where you want to be
with **teach yourself**

For UK order enquiries: please contact Bookpoint Ltd, 130 Milton Park, Abingdon, Oxon OX14 4SB. Telephone: +44 (0) 1235 827720. Fax: +44 (0) 1235 400454. Lines are open 09.00–18.00, Monday to Saturday, with a 24-hour message answering service. Details about our titles and how to order are available at www.teachyourself.co.uk

For USA order enquiries: please contact McGraw-Hill Customer Services, PO Box 545, Blacklick, OH 43004-0545, USA. Telephone: 1-800-722-4726. Fax: 1-614-755-5645.

For Canada order enquiries: please contact McGraw-Hill Ryerson Ltd, 300 Water St, Whitby, Ontario L1N 9B6, Canada. Telephone: 905 430 5000. Fax: 905 430 5020.

Long renowned as the authoritative source for self-guided learning – with more than 40 million copies sold worldwide – the **teach yourself** series includes over 300 titles in the fields of languages, crafts, hobbies, business, computing and education.

British Library Cataloguing in Publication Data: a catalogue record for this title is available from the British Library.

Library of Congress Catalog Card Number: on file.

First published in UK 2005 by Hodder Education, 338 Euston Road, London, NW1 3BH.

First published in US 2005 by Contemporary Books, a Division of the McGraw-Hill Companies, 1 Prudential Plaza, 130 East Randolph Street, Chicago, IL 60601 USA.

This edition published 2005.

The **teach yourself** name is a registered trade mark of Hodder Headline.

Copyright © 2005 APDT

Typeset by Transet Limited, Coventry, England.
Printed in Great Britain for Hodder Education, a division of Hodder Headline, 338 Euston Road, London NW1 3BH, by Cox & Wyman Ltd, Reading, Berkshire.

Hodder Headline's policy is to use papers that are natural, renewable and recyclable products and made from wood grown in sustainable forests. The logging and manufacturing processes are expected to conform to the environmental regulations of the country of origin.

Impression number   10 9 8 7 6 5 4 3 2 1
Year   2010 2009 2008 2007 2006 2005

acknowledgements

In memory of John Fisher

The APDT would like to pay special thanks to
Anita Stafford-Allen for providing the
artwork for this book

the authors

Introduction written by CC Guard

Chapter 1 written by Paddy Driscoll

Chapter 2 written by Carrie Evans

Chapter 3 written by Stella Bagshaw

Chapter 4 written by Barry Eaton

Chapter 5 written by Patsy Parry

Chapter 6 written by Julia Harbord, Geraldine Thomas, Sandra Fraser, Pauline Wise, Val Harvey, Stella Bagshaw

Chapter 7 written by Julia Harbord

Chapter 8 written by Barry Eaton and Sarah Whitehead

Chapter 9 and 10 written by Barry Eaton

Chapter 11 written by Pauline Wise and Sandra Fraser

Chapter 12 written by Stella Bagshaw

contents

introduction

History of the Association of Pet Dog Trainers

The Association of Pet Behaviour Councillors (APBC) was formed in 1989, the media acclaimed it the approach of the 'new style' dog training for the pet owning masses. The bringing of the 'why' into training.

Although the Behaviourists dealt with the one-to-one aspect, usually of aggressive dogs, where were they to send the man in the street with the uncomplicated dog? Pet owners did not need the precision of competition type training, but a dog that came when called, did not pull on the lead, or jump up and behaved in a socially acceptable manner with other dogs and humans.

In 1992 at the APBC symposium, the idea of the Association of Pet Dog Trainers (APDT) was put to the audience of 500 and was warmly received. In 1993 the APBC symposium announced the criteria for membership of the APDT. This was followed by a wave of protest. Assess everyone who wanted to join? Who would assess the Assessors? Because of the potential size of the task ahead, it was decided that the APDT should be completely independent. Pet Dog Trainers would organize their own house.

After an inaugural meeting in 1993 at Grantham, John Fisher (of Working Trails experience) became the APDT founder and chief executive. Through the magazine, *Dogs Today*, he ran a survey to find out what pet owners wanted. He asked for those who would be interested in the formation of the APDT to contact him with a view to setting up a national body.

Questionnaires were sent out. Over 500 forms were completed and returned. The overwhelming verdict was that all potential members should be assessed actually doing their job in their own venues – before joining the APDT.

Sixty people throughout the country were selected through John's personal knowledge of their activities, or other highly respected people in the dog world, to be the first assessors. These 60 elected a steering group by postal ballot for five people to lay foundations and report back. This steering group arranged draft copies of the Code of Practice, Constitution, application forms, etc.

The Kennel Club got a bit hot under the collar at this stage. Once it was pointed out that *individuals* became members of the APDT not *clubs*, they relaxed and have worked with the APDT, using some of their services ever since.

The official launch for the press was on 4 February 1994 at a Kensington hotel in London. Grayling & Co arranged the proceedings on behalf of Pedigree Petfoods and designed the original logo.

In August 1994 John Fisher sent out a co-coordinators' letter explaining how assessments were to be carried out. Since then the number of assessors has continued to be built up, after a stringent examination of their qualifications and training methods.

May 1994 saw the final meeting of assessors at Sheffield. Vets would be able to refer clients with confidence to members of the APDT. The overall aim of the Association would be to promote *kind, fair and effective* methods throughout the world of dog training.

The first Annual General Meeting (AGM) was held in September 1995 in Cambridgeshire, when the steering group handed over to the first elected Committee according to the constitution. C. C. Guard was elected as Chairman, John Fisher and Sarah Whitehead were to be executives in charge of developing the future of the APDT. At last the APDT was able to offer pet owners a guarantee of quality when looking for a training class or help with training a difficult dog in the area where they lived.

The second AGM was held at Hartbury College, unfortunately John Fisher was taken ill and sadly died of a malignant brain tumour on 18 February and C. C. Guard took over the full time running of the administrative office. Great responsibility was put on both her and Sarah Whitehead to continue nurturing John's baby into adolescence.

Members of the APDT were assessed according to the strict Code of Practice drawn up by the members themselves at the AGM and contain the words

> condemning such equipment as check/choke chains, prong or spike collars, electric shock devices in any form, and high frequency sound devices which are designed to startle.

All prospective members of the APDT still undergo a thorough testing, consisting of a questionnaire and a visit by an assessor to see the applicant working in a practical situation, training pet owners in their own venues. If the applicant meets the criteria and has agreed to abide by the APDT Code of Practice, the administrative office then issues a certificate, membership number and the entitlement to use the logo. One undertaking members abide by is to continue their further training and education, thereby acquiring new knowledge of theory and practice. This is checked on each year when renewing membership.

Those who are not quite ready to join the APDT, or are not running classes may join the Subscribers' List. This gives them three newsletters a year, a county print-out, and with the politeness of a phone call subscribers can visit other members' classes to observe. They can join the library scheme making full use of all the videos and books and have reduced fees at any events run by the APDT.

The first newsletter went out in Spring 1995. Membership by subscription started on this date, with 86 members, the first renewal date to be 1996.

Several members have joined the APDT from France, Italy, Eire, Northern Ireland, Japan, Greece, Canada and the USA.

Summer 1995 saw the first directory printed by the APDT. It was realized that sponsorship would be needed in future to meet the expenses that were not covered by membership fees. Now veterinary surgeons receive an annual APDT directory of all members in county order. This can be used to help pet owners select a trainer that is guaranteed to use kind, fair and effective methods. Vets usually ask for more directories, one for each of their clinics.

After Pedigree Petfoods' initial help, Arden Grange stepped into the breach and printed directories for both 1997 and 1998. Hills

International covered the next three years and now James Wellbeloved has taken over the reins. Four thousand directories are printed every year.

Over the years the APDT has built up a database of over 4,000 practising vets with the help of the APDT members in each vet's area. The friends' database covers charities, libraries, colleges, breeders and Citizen Advice Bureaus.

All veterinary personnel can rest assured that every APDT member is happy to work closely with the referring practice, in whatever way they are requested to do so. Members have to carry public liability insurance and if offering behaviour advice must also have personal indemnity insurance.

Any pet owner contacting the administrative office, enquiring about classes, is given access to an up-to-date county print-out giving names, addresses and telephone numbers of members in their areas. This also includes details of other services a member may offer. Pet owners can be certain that no coercive or punitive techniques and equipment will be used by members.

The APDT has held several very successful workshops and activity weekends over the years. Workshops are also held annually by members in Scotland and Wales for the general public and members alike. The APDT also runs courses recognized by the Open College Network (OCN). The APDT receives constant enquiries from people interested in becoming trainers or taking courses. This information can also be supplied by the administrative office.

The APDT has had a presence at Crufts for the past four years. Situated in Hall 1 the red banners mark the stand from all directions. Several other shows have an APDT presence, supported by several members from the area.

The APDT is not in competition with any other organization and all trainers use slightly different techniques when helping pet owners with problems and to train their own dogs. Rest assured that APDT members use methods of training that are the *kind, fair and effective* way of training dogs throughout the British Isles.

01

principles of dog training

In this chapter you will learn:
- what makes your dog tick
- how to motivate your dog
- how to train effectively.

How dogs learn

At the beginning

From the day your dog was born he was learning. From the very first struggle to find a teat to get milk, the very first attempts at play, the first squeal or bark, what happened as a consequence was beginning to dictate how that pup was going to develop into an adult dog. By the time you got your pup at seven or eight weeks old the learning had already started, and his early rearing and development will have already had an impact. If you had taken on an adult dog then more 'learned' behaviour is firmly established, good and bad. Whatever the age of dog you have taken on, you aren't starting with a blank sheet.

The genetic input

The genes your dog was born with make a difference to how he responds to or learns from events. Dogs are usually born with 'breed' specific characteristics; for example, German shepherds are more likely to want to guard and retrievers are more likely to want to carry articles around. Some may be less obvious, like cavalier King Charles spaniels who can have strong retrieving instincts; a remnant of their gundog ancestry. Dogs also have specific traits inherited from both the dam and the sire. It might be something as insignificant as about the way a dog cocks his head or barks. But it can also be a tendency to be aggressive, energetic, and obsessive or some other characteristic. These kinds of characteristics can influence how easily your dog learns and what you might need to teach him.

It is debatable how much we humans have altered the original 'wolf', but there are plenty of traits that have been enhanced either by accident or design, which suit us. Some traits have been weakened, either by 'natural selection' or by our active intervention, and some have been enhanced.

Border collies, for instance, have been bred for many generations to want to work obsessively and be very single minded in their work. They have been bred to have ultra-high speed reactions. But these traits, whilst excellent for training for competitive sports like agility, for example, can make life difficult in an average family home and a Border collie in a domestic situation needs a lot of investment in training and exercise. A dog which has been bred for many generations to display very strong genetic traits is going to be hard to train to stop displaying them, whether it's a springer spaniel wanting to put his nose down and search or a terrier wanting to kill small furry creatures.

But on the other hand we have developed plenty of breeds that have their chase and hunting instincts reduced (but never removed entirely), for example the French bulldog, the rough collie or the Newfoundland. A liking for dogs as cute, possibly even precocious, companions, which don't demand huge amounts of exercise, has led us to breed some dogs, like many toy breeds such as the bichon frise, or the toy or miniature poodles. They are likely to be less single minded than the average Border collie, but are likely to be more 'creative' and independent. Neither temperament is better or easier than the other to train, just different.

Some breeds have more specific behaviours, which may have happened almost by accident. Many of the spitz breeds (but not all) have a strong tendency towards barking, for instance. You will find it a lot harder to teach your average Finnish or German spitz to be quiet than your average English setter.

However, it's not all bad news. It's these very traits that can make training easier for us if we use them to our advantage. The basic instincts for hunting and chasing as well as the desire to be part of a social group, all make our jobs easier.

What these traits mean is you can have an expectation of how your dog might behave. It helps you predict what his training needs might be in addition to those you have identified already. But don't let your preconceptions about what you are told about your dog's breed, or genes, limit you and what you want to teach your dog to do. One of the greatest disservices owners do to their dogs is in assuming their 'breed' is different to all other dogs and therefore cannot learn certain things.

Of course, if you have a rescue dog of unknown parentage you have no helpful pointers except guesswork. It adds to the fun of training; trying to work out where your dog's traits might have come from and what breeds can be detected. But at the end of the day it doesn't matter. Your dog is a unique and independent animal who is his own 'person' and that is the dog you are training. You aren't training a collection of genes.

Vive la différence

You probably realize no two dogs are the same. Also what you want from your dog is going to be different to another family. It is for *you* to decide what you want out of training your dog and although this book covers the 'basics' you may not want to teach your dog all of them. That's fine! The collective experience of APDT members is that these are the exercises that are most asked for and needed by dog owners. But training isn't just about following a recipe and following instructions. It's about understanding *your* dog and matching his and your needs.

For instance, if your dog is very lively and energetic and you would like him to be calmer, you might want to teach him to relax and settle down before you teach him to fetch a ball for instance. Whereas if you have a more laid back puppy you might want to put more emphasis on teaching him to want to run about and play games before you worry about teaching him a sit stay.

The human/canine interface

The basic 'blueprint' of the wolf is often used as a model of how we should train our dogs. Dogs do share basic behaviours with wolves and other *canids*, and we ignore them at our peril! Most pet dogs have some tendency to want to chase, growl, dig and compete for food, for example, whatever the breed. But the importance of understanding a wild wolf pack structure in *teaching* our family pet dogs how to behave in our human world is largely overstated. Dogs can only come with 'dog' behaviour, which is genetically very 'wolf like', that is true, but that doesn't help our pet dogs understand and learn human language and behaviour. Every dog has to *learn* every human signal or command. We humans can only be 'human'. Our values, language and development are different. Dogs cannot emulate people. Dogs can never learn a human 'moral' outlook. It is doubtful that they ever learn our language other than as 'cues' to actions or consequences. They can only learn the meaning of a word such as 'sit', for example, if we then teach them that if they then put their bottom on the floor, that action has a consequence. And if they *don't* put their bottom on the floor when asked, *that* has a consequence too.

Even when your dog understands those cues or commands, he then has to want to do as asked. Dogs, like us, will work to gain things they want, or work to avoid things they don't like. The APDT ethos is to train with the former, and work hard to avoid the latter. Dogs learn to do things (or stop doing things) through what is advantageous to them and what is disadvantageous. They can never learn it is 'wrong', in a moral sense, to bite people or chase livestock, or that is 'right' to come when called or not jump up.

Control the environment

The job we have in training our dogs is to help them understand what we want of them, taking the trouble to understand what they are saying to us. It shouldn't be a one way 'me master–you slave' relationship, but one of you has to be in control of events and if it's the dog, then you are in trouble! The knack in training is for you, the owner, to control the environment in which your dog lives. To supply consequences to actions, and manage things so your dog cannot get things terribly wrong. And finally, to teach him the meanings of certain words and signals.

Training will never teach your dog to stop wanting to behave like a dog. Dogs are independent, thinking creatures with motivations and emotions that all too often conflict with what we want of them. You must be realistic about your expectations. Dogs have natural drives, which demand they find food and find a mate. All training does is shift the odds in your favour that you can stop your dog following those drives when you don't want him to. Castrating a male dog will dramatically improve those odds if he is fighting other male dogs or escaping in order to look for bitches. But don't let those expectations limit you and what you can try and achieve. You may not get a 100 per cent reliable recall from a lurcher, but if you don't try, you won't succeed.

Some training techniques rely on punishing dogs for unwanted, but natural, dog behaviours, but it is invariably better to manage things so your dog cannot do them, or teach him an alternative behaviour which can be rewarded. One luxury we pet dog owners have is that we *can* control our dog's environment and we can, by using leads, fences and doors limit our dogs' choices so they are not put at risk.

Motivation

Rewards

Many dog trainers and owners talk about 'rewards'. Technically speaking when we talk about rewards, we should be talking about 'reinforcement'. The psychology textbooks describe reinforcement as anything that 'increases, or strengthens, a behaviour'. Broadly speaking, reinforcement is what causes your dog to *choose* to repeat something like coming when called, or sitting when asked. But it's not just about us consciously supplying a reward as some kind of 'payment' for a correctly carried out action. Much of it is accidental. A dog is very quick to spot a situation which is to his benefit and it's one of the reasons why dogs have been so successful as a species in our human environment. For instance, a dog may sit close to you in the kitchen when you prepare food, if he comes to expect some scraps might fall on the floor. That 'sitting next to Mum' action is being *reinforced* by food falling on the floor.

A reinforcer, or reward, is usually something nice, like a food treat or a game or a fuss from an owner. On the whole, although there are exceptions, pet dogs and especially pups want attention, food and play. It's your *dog's* definition of reward that is important here, not yours, so you will need to know what turns your dog on. Special food treats are usually top of the list. Games may be more difficult as some dogs have to be taught how to enjoy playing, much like we need to if we are to enjoy a game, whether it's soccer, Monopoly or tug-of-war. But once learned, and used effectively, play can be a powerful reinforcer. Attention is usually desirable to a dog because it is often paired with something else. We tend to give them attention when we give them a game, or their dinner or a food treat. Some dogs like affection and a fuss, but it isn't usually high on the list of desirable rewards for the majority of dogs. It's often us owners who like giving a dog a stroke and a pat more than most dogs like receiving them!

Reinforcement isn't just about being 'nice' to your dog, it's about you giving one of those things, which your dog actively wants, as a consequence to your dog's action, which makes it more likely the action will be repeated in the future.

Practical application of 'reinforcement' (rewards)

How do you use 'reinforcement' in training your dog? Before you can give your dog a reward (and reinforce the behaviour), your puppy or dog has to do the action. You can't get your dog to do more of something if he isn't doing it in the first place!

There are different ways you can 'engineer' your dog into doing things so they can be reinforced. Luring with a food treat works best for some exercises, like a sit or a down, for instance. But your dog will need to learn (as will you) how to use a food lure effectively. It is not unusual for an adult dog that has never been trained using food to not want to follow a food lure, so he may take a little longer to learn. It can take a few attempts, but persevere since it will make so much of the training easier.

Using a food lure

Have some small tasty food treats. They can be chopped up hot dog, sausage, cheese or any other kind of 'real' food that your dog likes. Avoid using sugary dog treats since you could be giving your dog a lot of treats and they should be nutritionally valuable.

Hold one in the tips of your fingers as shown in Figure 1.

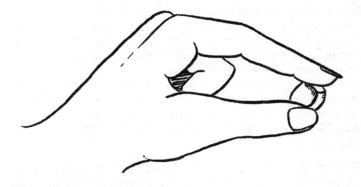

Fig 1 How to hold a dog treat

Stick to either the right or the left hand for now. Don't chop and change to start with. If you want to go on to do any kind of obedience competitions with your dog, or know you will be going into a class which progresses to that, it is probably best if you use the left hand, but otherwise it doesn't matter which.

Place the treat on your dog's nose so he can really get a good sniff of it. Using a very slow, very deliberate movement draw the food away and as your dog moves his nose to follow it, tell him he's 'good!' and let him take the treat. Open your hand up and allow him to take it from your palm, like you would feed a sugar lump to a pony. You might find it easier to just drop it onto the floor for him. You might even throw it into the air for him to catch! It doesn't much matter so long as your dog begins to learn that if he follows that hand holding the treat at some point you will let him have it. Repeat, and with each repetition expect him to move just a few more inches, a few more steps after the food before letting him have it. If you can picture it as your finger tips being like a magnet, with your dog's nose attached it can help.

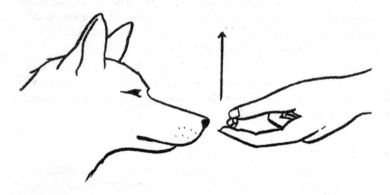

Fig 2 How to lure a dog with a good treat

Once he is confident about following the lure, start to move your dog with a bit more energy and with him showing some zest for this 'game'. One of the ways to stop training becoming boring is to bring a bit of movement into the picture, and how you move your dog with a food lure can help do that.

You can use a food lure for teaching your dog to:

- Sit
- Down
- Roll over
- Twirl
- Follow you.

Body language

Luring with food isn't the only way to get your dog to act in the way you want. The way you use your body language can work well and the chances are you are already doing that. For instance, in calling your dog to you, crouching down, running away or waving your arms may help induce your dog to come to you. Sometimes 'shaping' is the only way to teach your dog something. Chapter 06 looks at how to teach specific exercises and Chapter 08 looks at clicker training, which will cover some aspects of this. But the goal is always the same. Get your dog doing the action, somehow, and then reward him with a clear 'marker' as he does the action to tell him why he earned the reward. Since your dog has no knowledge of English, until taught, there is no point giving your dog a command until your dog can do the action. That comes later.

Effective training uses all of these methods to our advantage. Success not only relies on knowing what your dog wants though, but also being very clear in your communication what action earned the reward.

Play rewards

Whilst some dogs are naturally playful, others aren't. However, most dogs can learn to play and it's a good idea to teach them. The kind of games I am talking about are retrieving games, e.g. fetching a ball and tugging games – tugging on a rope tuggy toy. It is never a good idea to encourage your puppy to play by pulling at your clothes or chasing you and the children though, so steer clear of any games that encourages your dog to bite or chase people. Also, whatever games you play your dog needs to learn your rules, or he will make up his own and they may not be safe or good rules. An effective play reward is one where your dog interacts with you, with an article (e.g. a ball) between you. It should be a shared activity.

Why play?

Play can be an excellent reward in training. It exercises your dog so less behaviour problems are likely to happen. A tired dog wants to rest, not destroy the sofa or dig holes in the garden!

If you are going to use play as a reward in training you use it in the same way a food treat is used. Your dog does something correctly, you tell him 'good!', then he gets his opportunity for a game with you. You can give him a food treat as well if you like. Games are also very important for teaching your dog rules about how he should and shouldn't behave. For instance, expecting him to sit before he is given permission to go fetch a ball will teach your dog to control his instinctive desire to chase. Teaching him tuggie games teaches him some very important rules about when to bite, what to bite and to let go of things when asked.

Teaching 'fetch'

Chapter 06 looks at how to teach your dog to retrieve. For purposes of training, if you use fetching a toy as a reward, then it is important to keep it fun and the rules to a minimum. Throw the ball a long way, encouraging your dog to run back as fast as possible with it. If you have a young dog or a dog with any joint problems, you may want to check with your vet first that this amount of exercise is suitable for your dog.

Teaching tuggie

Some people avoid teaching their dogs to play tuggie as they believe it can make the dog aggressive. Don't worry. There is no evidence at all that this is the case. What it *does* do, however, is teach your dog essential rules about biting and giving up articles, so far from causing any problems, taught properly, it will prevent them. But it is important you stick to teaching your dog the rules or you could teach your dog to enjoy grabbing things he shouldn't.

The *big 3 rules* of tuggie games

1 If your dog takes the toy without permission, you stop the game. Only *you* start the game. Teach a command such as 'take it'. Although your dog must win the tuggie sometimes (or he will give up playing) you should end up with it, offering a food swap before you take it for the last time.

2 Your dog must not be able to run off with the tuggie. If needs be, put a trailing house-line or lead on him, which you can put your foot on to stop him running off with it should you inadvertently drop it. Or better still, make sure you have a better toy or food treat to trade for it. Don't chase him around for it!

3 You also need to teach him a cue that means 'let me have it', e.g. 'give'. Stop tugging the tuggie, swap the tuggie for a food treat, if he doesn't want to let it go, then start playing again. Teach him that when he gives you articles it doesn't inevitably mean the fun stops. If he is determined to not let you have the tuggie and hangs on, then put one hand in his collar, let go with your other hand so you are no longer holding the tuggie and wait patiently for him to drop it. Immediately he does, it is important to offer it back so you can restart the game. Repeat this until he realizes the only way to continue the game after you have said 'give' is to let the tuggie drop.

If your dog breaks the 'big' rules (grabbing you at any time or helping himself to the toy while you are holding it), stop the game completely, possibly for that day. Swap the tuggie for a small food treat then put it away. Beware of how you play tug with physically immature dogs or dogs with poor dentition.

Reward every time the dog gets something right

When you start to teach a particular exercise, to start with your dog needs to get a reward *every* time he gets it right. So if he sits when you lure him into a sit, he gets a reward. For every correct action your dog needs one of his tangible, desired rewards. A bit of sausage, the opportunity to run after a ball, or the chance to run off lead in the park. It doesn't matter what the reward is, so long as your dog actively wants it. The one reward that we humans like to give, but is usually the least effective, is just verbal praise on its own. We overvalue it enormously. In reality the words mean nothing to your dog *except* what he has learned they mean. Which isn't 'I really approve of what you have just done'. You might well approve, but that's not the point as far as your dog is concerned! To your dog it ought to mean 'well done! You got it right and here's what you *really* want … your dinner, a treat, a game …'. Sadly, it can mean, with more traditional correction based training, 'well done! You just avoided a smack, a jerk on the choke chain, or a telling off …'. Verbal praise on its own will not work long term unless it is paired with a desired consequence for your dog.

Teaching the command or 'cue'

Once you can predict your dog will reliably follow the lure, and will reliably do the action you are teaching without hesitation, and hopefully with some speed and commitment, then and only then, do you introduce your word of command or 'cue'. Decide in advance what that command is to be (see Chapter 04). Say it just *before* you start the luring action, count to two, then move your hand to lure your dog into position. Once he is in position, praise, and then give him the food treat as you have been doing over the last few sessions. Your dog is appearing to 'obey' your command, but he has absolutely no idea what the word means, or even that it has any significance at first. If you say 'down', then he lies down because you have lured him, don't be fooled into thinking he has understood that 'down' means lay on the ground. He hasn't. Not yet!

Repeat that sequence of command, pause, action, reward over a few sessions, and you may find that your dog begins to realize if he hears that sound ('down'), if he performs that action where he lies on the ground, a reward appears. When he starts to lie down before you start to lure, and it may be a very half-hearted attempt, you know he is *beginning* to understand! So the first time that happens, give him double rations, maybe three, and make a great fuss of him. But you may need to take a more planned approach to dispensing with the food lure.

Once your dog begins to understand your commands but is inconsistent, or doesn't obey another member of the family, it may be worth considering what your dog understands by your word of command. It isn't the word itself. A dog may not understand if the word 'sit' becomes 'sit down' in the next breath, or is said by a person with an entirely different tone of voice or accent. Sound cross and your dog may not recognize it, so the scenario where you, the owner, gets crosser and crosser (and probably louder and louder) might mean your dog stands less and less chance of getting it right. If your dog does not understand, raising your voice and sounding 'firm' will not help. It's like shouting or speaking slower to a foreigner who has no knowledge of English. Shouting does not aid understanding. The word 'sit' itself has no meaning for your dog, only that particular sound. Vary that sound and your dog may have no idea what you are asking of him. Don't be too quick to assume he is disobeying you. He may simply not understand.

Dispensing with the food lure

Unless you want to spend the rest of your dog's life using food to lure him into these positions, at some point your dog needs to understand it isn't just following the food that is getting you to give the food to him, it's the *action* he is doing that works to get the desired consequence, i.e. that food treat. Food lure/reward training can easily go wrong if you don't get that important message across to your dog.

Give your verbal command or cue. Start to lure as you have been doing up to now. But *this* time instead of luring your dog all the way into position, at the last minute, quickly and decisively take your hand out of the way. Take it behind your back and make it disappear so your dog can't follow it any more. If you have done enough repetitions of the whole action and time it right, your dog can't help but continue moving into the position you want him in whether it be a 'down' or a 'sit'. At this point *immediately* put your hand back again and give him the reward. In this training session repeat this a few times, each time whisking your hand away sooner and sooner so your dog completes the action without the lure on his nose. With each repetition, take slightly longer to put your hand back to reward him, and if he moves to follow your hand, whisk it away again. If he steadfastly refuses to go back into the position you asked for, go back to luring a few more times, then try removing the treat again. Mix them up a bit. Some are lured all the way, some you don't. Reward the latter ones better.

Fig 3 How to dispense with a food lure

In the final stage you will only move your hand slightly towards
your dog after your command. You are watching and waiting
for your dog to make the decision for himself to lie down. It
may be hesitant, because he no longer has the prop the lure
offers him, but should he make the decision to lie down, reward
him well.

Bribery?

You should also be getting into a habit of training without food
in your hand unless it's necessary. If your dog's 'obedience'
depends on you having food in your hand, then your dog is only
half trained. It can become a prop for both you and your dog!

At the stage where your dog is just beginning to understand a
word of command, it is *essential* that he continues to get the
reward for doing the action every time when you don't have
food in your hand, or he will learn that if you don't have food
in your hand he is never rewarded. This is when a lot of dogs
start to only 'obey' you when you have food, and not when you
don't. From the dog's point of view it makes perfect sense. No
food in hand = no reward. So why bother? It is important that
the presence (or absence) of food in your hand becomes
irrelevant. That rewards may appear when he carries out the
action. It is not dependent on whether or not they are in your
hand. It is far too easy for your dog to see the food as part of
the 'cue' (or command) and when he stops doing as asked when
you don't have food he isn't being 'crafty' or disobedient or
stubborn, he is simply not understanding that you have changed
the rules and the cue.

Similarly with all the paraphernalia that goes with a training
session. Don't use them! Bum bags, plastic bags, visible rewards
all tell your dog this time 'we're training'. Go out into the real
world without those clear visual aids and he stops believing he
is still supposed to be complying with commands and that his
good behaviour will be rewarded. This is a mistake. Remember,
your dog cannot know you expect the same responses
everywhere unless you supply the same consequences
everywhere.

Moving on

After a few training sessions on a particular exercise you are
likely to be able to say your word of command, and your dog
should be responding, without a luring action, which you are

rewarding every time. You are progressing well! But no one wants to have to carry food around, or throw a ball every time the dog complies with a command. From a training point of view it's actually not very effective since experiments have shown that for an animal (whether human or dog) to respond well long term it is important to then vary how and when the rewards appear. A lottery is a very good example of how it works. How many people who come up with the action of going to the shop and buying a lottery ticket get a reward every time? Not many! But week in, week out, they do as the adverts suggest. Go buy a lottery ticket. It's because they *know* that the action *might* at some point have the consequence of a huge amount of money coming their way. The smaller lottery prizes, earned randomly and not in themselves very valuable, keep that belief alive. The principle of randomly rewarding the action is an essential part of the training.

Now your dog understands which action results in the reward after a certain cue ('sit', 'down', 'buy a lottery ticket', whatever), you need to change *how* you reward. You don't reduce the rewards; just change how your dog receives them. So this time ask your dog to carry out the action, praise him, and release him from that action without giving him a treat. The chances are he will look at you expectantly, wondering where the treat is. Pretend you haven't noticed, and then ask him to carry out the action again. He should do it. His belief that you are going to reward him may be a little dented, but he should still be willing to come up with the appropriate action. Reward that one with *extra* treats. Some for the first response you *didn't* reward, plus some for that second response. Next time ask for two successful responses before you reward him. But next time reward him for the *first* attempt again. It is a mistake at this stage to make it more and more difficult to earn the treats. It's more important to keep him guessing which attempt will earn him the 'prize'. Sometimes it's the first attempt, sometimes the third. Over a few training sessions you gradually extend the number of successful repetitions of the action the dog is willing to do before you part with the rewards, which get bigger and better, the more you ask of him. Over time, you may only reward, tangibly, every tenth or twentieth successful response to a 'sit' command, but boy, is the reward good! Ten throws of the ball. The dog's entire dinner. Being let off lead for a good run in the park with friends. You will help maintain the dog's strong and reliable response to a command by sometimes giving smaller, lower value rewards in between. Verbal praise, a stroke, a small bit of boring dog biscuit ... all will help remind your dog he has got it right, but if he wants the 'jackpot' he just has to keep on coming up with that behaviour for a few more times. He must start to believe that *next* time is the time he will get the doggy equivalent of £23 million!

Outdoors ... the 'real world!'

In all training there is an element of just making sure you build up good habits and routines. That your dog learns what 'sit' is and what you 'do' when the lead is being put on. That 'standing still' is what you 'do' when you produce a towel to dry him. Where there is no conflicting motivation often the rewards can be minimal or virtually zero and you may not even be aware there is 'learning' going on. If the alternative to sitting still and getting dinner as a consequence, is doing nothing, then it's an easy decision for the dog to make. Dinner or nothing? Hardly a difficult choice is it?

However, one of the biggest problems you will have is getting your dog to respond out in the 'real world'. The 'real world' is wherever you take your dog where he is going to meet other dogs, noise, traffic, kids playing football, cats, bikes, open spaces, etc. The distractions are huge and the alternatives to doing as asked are usually vastly more attractive to your dog. At home, it is very easy for your dog to learn a lot of the things you want to teach him. But outside is a different kettle of fish!

Dogs are very conscious of contexts. If he never gets rewarded in certain places for doing certain actions, then he will stop doing them. Also, remember his 'obedience' isn't a moral decision on his part to comply because he thinks you are a more important 'dog' than him (wolves don't go round issuing commands to other wolves), it's a result of you conditioning him to respond to specific commands which become predictors of certain consequences. If you reward a sit at home with a food treat, and never reward him at all when you are out then he will only comply with your commands at home and not when you are out. Which is when so many owners start to believe the dog needs to be told off, or forced into complying. In reality you just need to take the time and trouble to reinforce what you want everywhere, not just in the front room, your garden or the dog training class.

Assuming your dog understands your commands at home, you then have to virtually re-teach that command in other places. If your dog takes little notice of you when you ask him to do something outside, it is not that he has stopped 'understanding' commands, nor is he being naughty, stubborn or disobedient if he doesn't do as asked. It is that the alternatives have become irresistible. He just needs to learn that the commands he has learnt at home still have the same meaning outside and that once a cue has been given there is no point thinking about doing anything else because no alternative action will work to produce any kind of reward for him. That is up to you to manage! Once you have asked him to 'sit' or 'come', it's up to you to make sure it's not possible for him to do something else instead, and worse, have that incorrect action reinforced. Of course, it's important you have taught each command really well at home first. Unless he will respond reliably and with distractions at home, don't even consider trying to use those commands in the park, or on the street. All too often an owner expects a dog to come back in the park when they haven't even taught it at home. If your dog doesn't come in from the garden, from any room in the house, immediately and fast, every time you call, it is unfair and unreasonable to expect him to in the park. You must teach your dog at home first everything you are going to ask of him outside.

When you do go outdoors, whatever exercise you are teaching him, initially keep your dog on a lead, or a long line, and start with your food lures, or however you originally succeeded in teaching him at home, then reward him generously for doing as asked. He must believe that the rules are the same. If he comes up with an action, on a particular cue, or command, then good things happen for him. If you can't get him to respond, because he is too excited, or distracted, take him to a quieter place, with fewer distractions and where it is easier to get a good result. Take it gradually, not expecting too much too soon. Whether you have a pup or an older dog, the same rules apply. Make it easy to start with in every new place, get success, and then reward him. You might need to have extra special food treats. Or train outside just before the dog's normal feeding time so he is a bit hungrier than he would be just after. Take his favourite toy and play with him. You have a lot of competition for his attention outside, so be ready for it and make sure that if there was a contest for 'who can win the dog's attention' you would win it. You can't force your dog to prefer you over a group of playful puppies or chasing squirrels, so you have to persuade him that you are really a much better bet and have everything those pups can offer, plus interest. This is where his genes are going to become more evident, as well as his early rearing. Some dogs are more gregarious than others. Some want to chase more than others. You will have to work harder at teaching and motivating your dog if he is one of them, and while you are training, keep him under control either on a lead or a line.

It is important for your dog to learn that once you have asked for a certain action (e.g. 'come'), then only that action will result in a good consequence for him. Once you have called him, it must not be possible for him to run off and play with other dogs, or chase squirrels. That is where you need to manage things properly. Putting him on a long line so he *can't* go off and chase them will do the trick. Every time you give a command and your dog comes up with an alternative action, which is then strongly rewarded (for example being able to run off and play with other dogs when you have said 'come'), you are undoing all the good work you have done so far.

Worse, if you do that often enough, the cue you intend to mean one thing can come to mean exactly the opposite to your dog! It is not unusual to meet dogs who when they hear their owners say 'Fido! Come!' run off after other dogs, because that is what they believe is what you 'do'. If they hear the cue 'come', then go off and play, a very strong reinforcer, 'come' becomes a cue to run off and play. The dog that does that, far from being disobedient, is actually doing exactly what the owner has taught. Remember, obedience is not to do with the dog having an understanding of what words mean, but what they 'cue' and what the consequences are when they hear that word.

For training to work effectively in the outside world you need to work through the 'teaching' stage at home so the dog understands the meaning of the cues or commands. When you start training outside you need to be in control of events so your dog can't 'mislearn' or be too easily seduced by the alternatives. It's no use allowing your dog to get it wrong and you getting cross with him when it is totally within your power to make sure it doesn't go wrong.

Over a period of time, which could be days, weeks or months (depending on the dog and the exercise you are trying to teach), you need to gradually work on each exercise in slightly more distracting environments. Whether you are training a puppy or an adult dog, *every* outing is about training your dog. It's like learning to drive. You start off learning how to get the car to work and what actions you need to carry out in a quiet area, slowly concentrating on the task in hand. You don't expect to go out for a drive on a busy motorway or in busy town traffic until you have mastered the basics in quiet back roads.

Off lead

At some point you will realize you don't need the lead or line on your dog when training outside and that he complies with your requests to do things without any help or prompting from you. Well done! Safety and the law rather than his level of training will dictate whether or not he is on lead. Of course you must never have your dog off lead near roads or livestock and there is no kudos in showing off how well trained your dog is by letting that happen. If in doubt, be careful and keep him on lead.

Negative reinforcement and punishment

Sometimes 'negative reinforcement' is used in training whereby something unpleasant is *removed* in order to get a dog to repeat an action. Like the unpleasant noise a buzzer makes in your car if you haven't put on your seat belt. It causes you to put your seat belt on in order to switch off the unpleasant sound of that buzzer. An example of this in dog training is to put physical pressure on the dog's rear end to get him to sit, and when he sits, your hand is removed. But it is unlikely you will need to use any 'negative reinforcement' in training your dog. It usually means the dog has to avoid something it doesn't like in order to get a reward.

The word 'punishment' conjures up all sorts of bad images and ideas, mostly justified. Scientifically speaking 'punishment' is anything that reduces the likelihood an action will happen again. Notice I say *'reduces'*. Punishments, like smacking, shaking or shouting never eliminate actions altogether, only removing the 'reinforcement' (rewards) will do that. For instance, to reduce excessive puppy play biting, the very simple consequence of you stopping playing with the pup is very effective. You are no longer 'reinforcing' (rewarding) the puppy's biting by continuing to play. If you were to smack or shake your pup for play biting it might well stop him doing it at that moment, but it can be just about the worst thing you can do from a long-term training and behaviour point of view. You are likely to get any number of other results in addition to your pup stopping playing at that moment. Your pup may start to fear you. He may start to avoid your hands. Worse, he may bite harder because he feels he has to defend himself from being 'attacked' by you. He may just think what you are doing is part of the game and it could make him wilder, and bite harder. But most importantly, he won't learn 'bite inhibition' (see Chapter 05) which you may not be aware of until he is an adult, maybe years down the line. Punishments involving you, the owner, being nasty to your dog, or being aggressive, are *never* a good idea.

Punishment also has a nasty habit of escalating to abuse. Punishment can cause stress, anxiety, pain, insecurity and mistrust. As a general rule, punishments, especially physical corrections, have no place in modern dog training. There is almost invariably an alternative, desired behaviour you can 'reinforce' which will remove the need to be unpleasant to your dog. If there isn't, then managing things so your dog can't go wrong is usually a preferred option. If your dog is in the position where you feel only a smack or a shake will work then it suggests you probably need to manage things better. If your dog is taking food from a kitchen worktop, rather than smacking your dog, why not just shut the door? Or keep food out of his reach? There is no shame in avoiding situations where you could find yourself damaging the relationship between you and your dog.

Inadvertent learning and motivation

It's worth emphasizing that dogs are learning through both reinforcement and punishment all the time, whether or not you are involved and they may not be learning what we think they are! Also they learn unwanted behaviour just as easily as wanted. Remember, your dog has no human 'moral' rule book to go by, just a lot of dog genes, which drive a lot of what he wants to do.

Inadvertent consequences

Understand what is 'reinforcing' your dog's actions might be critical to sorting out behaviour problems he might have. Take 'jumping up' for instance. If your dog is jumping up at people, or you, then it is very likely that the person he is jumping up at is looking at, or touching, or fussing him. Since most dogs like attention, then this is highly likely to be 'reinforcing' the jumping up behaviour, even if he is being told 'Naughty boy! Get off!' the attention and touching is making the problem worse, not better. If something happens which your dog likes then he will do it again. Later chapters look at dealing with problems like jumping up, but if you can understand the basic principle that dogs will repeat actions that are rewarded it does not take a great leap of logic to work out that they will stop those actions if they are no longer rewarded. Often a 'problem' comes from the actions your dog is carrying out being inadvertently reinforced (rewarded), if not by you, by someone else or something in the environment.

Similarly, inadvertent 'punishment' may be stopping your dog doing something you want him to do. For instance, it is very common for owners to put the dog's lead on and finish a walk after they've called their dog to them. Even worse, some tell their dog off for running away in the first place. Unsurprisingly, before long, their dog might avoid returning to the owner. From the dog's point of view, going back to the owner results in unwanted consequences. Having the walk end and being shouted at. If your dog likes to run about off lead and hates being shouted at, why on earth would he return to you? He'd be stupid to, and dogs are rarely stupid!

Conclusion

You have your dog, genes and all. If he is an adult, he will have more years of 'learning' behind him than a young pup. But even an old dog can learn new tricks. Age is no barrier to learning although it may take longer to change old, unwanted behaviour. You dog's type or breed may influence how he learns and his attitude to learning, but it should never be an excuse for not teaching him things he can learn and enjoy.

He needs to be taught every human signal and command carefully and positively, through training. In the words of dog trainer Joanna Hill 'if a dog doesn't do as he is asked, then he either doesn't understand or he isn't motivated enough to want to do it'. Both are within our power to change.

For a few sessions, which may be hours, days or it may be longer depending on your dog and what sessions you are trying to teach, give the dog a reward every time for carrying out the action.

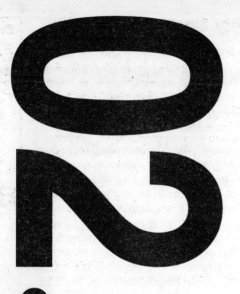

02

equipment

In this chapter you will learn:
- how to find the right equipment for your dog
- how to fit a head collar properly
- how to find the right kind of lead for your dog.

Collars and identity tags

By law a dog should *always* wear a collar with an identification tag attached that has the owner's contact telephone number. It is a requirement by law and carries a £2000 fine for non-compliance. Many owners like to put their dog's name and their home address on, however, this has disadvantages and therefore is generally not recommended. Dog thefts are becoming more widespread and if your dog has his name on it, then it gives dog thieves a chance to make friends with him by using his own name. Ensure that your dog's collar fits correctly; it should be securely fitted to prevent him slipping out of it. If it is fitted correctly you should be able to fit 2–3 fingers comfortably between the collar and your dog's neck. A collar that is too loose will slip over his head, whereas a collar that is too tight will cause rubbing and sores.

Regularly check the identity tag to ensure that it is still readable. Your dog must still have an identification tag even if he has been micro chipped.

A collar can be made of leather or nylon fabric and will have either a buckle fastening or plastic quick release clip.

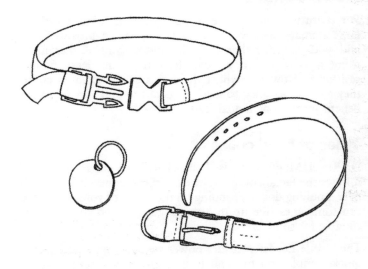

Fig 4 Various collars and an ID tag

Touching the collar

People tend to grab dogs by their collar. This is not always a sensible thing to do as sometimes dogs react defensively to this. However, it may happen, either with you or your family or a stranger. It is fair to say that your dog is going to have to have his collar felt and held to restrain him at sometime in his life, i.e. at the vets. It makes far more sense to teach him that being grabbed by the collar is a pleasant thing to happen. To do this, first touch his collar and reward him with high value rewards, something he really loves; then grab his collar a bit quicker this time and again reward him highly. Then grab his collar and give him a reward, pull him towards you, give him a reward and tell him he is a good boy.

When you call him to you, touch his collar before you reward him. Obviously, do not grab so quickly you frighten him, but teach him that this is a pleasant thing to happen. It is important that you get other people to touch his collar and not just you. For the vets, groomers' and anyone else's sake who may have to handle him in this way.

Head collars

For centuries people have understood that using a bridle on large animals, such as a cow or horse, has enabled us to steer and guide it rather than it pulling out of control, therefore by using a head collar we can lead from the least point of resistance. However, whilst these aids offer increased control, they are not designed to teach dogs not to pull and are of great benefit when using a dual-lead approach.

Types of head collar

Dr Roger Mugford devised the Halti head collar; it naturally follows the facial contours. The Halti exerts maximum steering over a pulling dog. Depending on the shape of your dog's face it can sometimes ride up into the dog's eyes and so may not be suitable for some breeds.

The Gentle Leader provides power steering and makes training quick, simple and fun and is suitable for all breeds and sizes of dog.

The DogAlter is an adjustable head halter that has Velcro straps to get the perfect fit. Devised by George Greyson, a member of the APDT, it is an aid to help calm and control boisterous dogs.

The figure of eight usually has a padded noseband and is less popular than the Halti or Gentle Leader.

Introducing a head collar to your dog

Head collars can be very useful when overcoming a whole range of behaviour and training problems. Although there is a great deal of feeling that head collars are similar to muzzles, they are not and they do have their uses. The head collar will not stop your dog doing anything he usually does except pull! A head collar will not alter the dog's behaviour, but it gives more control and can give great peace of mind. However, it is very unfair to simply put the head collar on the dog and hope it will be all right. Time and care *must* be taken to ensure the dog likes wearing the head collar.

- First of all let the dog see, sniff and take titbits off the head collar.

- Teach the dog to put his nose through the nosepiece of the head collar for really tasty tiny titbits. All the time from now on as soon as the head collar is near him you need to tell him how wonderful he is. When you take the head collar away from him you switch off and ignore him for a while.

- When he is happy putting his nose in, gently slide the straps around his ears whilst he is eating the titbits but do not fasten the head collar.

- This time, ensuring you have some more titbits which he can eat with the head collar on, put the head collar on as above, fasten the clip and feed him some extra titbits before taking it off and then ignoring him.

- Repeat this for as many short periods as possible, gradually reducing the number of titbits he eats and increasing the time the head collar is on.

- When your dog is happy to wear the head collar because be knows it gives him your attention and titbits, you can extend the time even further.

- If at any time the dog tries to scratch at the head collar, try to distract him and reward him for stopping. This means you are trying to progress too quickly.

- Now that your dog is happy wearing the head collar you can begin using it when out on walks. Because you are not worried, and the dog likes wearing the head collar, the dog will find it easier to relax.

Not all dogs suit a head collar and if you have tried all the above and your dog still really dislikes the head collar, then there are other training aids that can help you while you are teaching your dog loose lead walking.

Fig 5 A gentle leader and a Halti head collar

Body harnesses

There are various harnesses available; some are designed to stop the dog pulling whereas others are simply another means of restraining the dog instead of using a collar. The 'no-pull' harnesses fit around the dog's shoulders and apply pressure against the chest, encouraging the dog to walk slower. These include the 'Easy Walker', 'Walk-rite', 'Lupi' and the 'Stop Pull'. Care should be taken with all harnesses that they do not cause under-arm burns and chaffing.

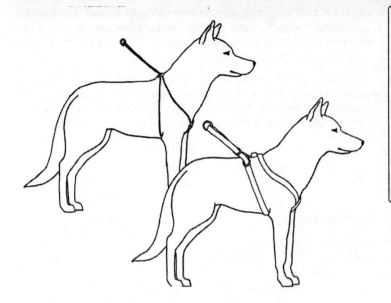

Fig 6 Various harnesses

Leads

It is important to regularly check the condition of your dog's lead. You will need to check the hook that attaches to the collar as it can become broken, damaged or jammed with mud and may cause the collar and lead to detach. Also check any stitching, checking for fraying or areas that the dog may have chewed. By regularly checking the dog's lead it will hopefully reduce the lead or collar breaking away at a critical moment.

What type of lead?

There are many different types of leads available and individual preference should be a priority. However, it is important to ensure that the lead is comfortable to hold and durable. You may choose a lead made of leather, rope, or one of the fancy fabric types. When choosing a lead it is important to consider the dog's size and strength as a lead that is too thin or has a clip that attaches to the collar that is too small could break easily. A dog that has a tendency to chew its lead might initially need a chain type; however, once the behaviour has been corrected a different type can be used. The soft nylon type leads are easy to clean and fit readily into pockets on walks when the dog is off the lead.

Many owners find extending leads helpful when teaching their dog to come when called or for dogs that cannot go off the lead. An extending lead is a long line, which is contained in the handle, and the handler controls the length of the lead. Whilst they are ideal for dogs that cannot go off the lead they *must* not be used near busy roads as the dog could cause an accident by suddenly walking into the road or in front of a person. Care must also be taken as the line can burn if allowed to slip through a person's hand, fingers, legs or feet.

Specialist leads

Double ended lead

Often called a 'training lead', this useful piece of equipment is usually about two metres in length with a G-clip at either end and several D-rings, which can be used to vary the length of the lead. It is a great benefit when using a dual-system approach with one G-clip attached to a head collar and the other to the dog's solid collar.

Indoor line or house line

The 'indoor line' or 'house line' facilitates teaching and training. This lightweight line of about 2 metres is attached to a non-slip collar – one that buckles or fastens and will not tighten up. It can either be held or allowed to trail behind the dog. The house-line can then be used to remove the dog from unwanted situations. Once new behaviours have become established the line can eventually be removed. However, it can be reintroduced at any time, should the need arise.

Garden line

A garden line is similar to a house-line and can be used to train a dog to come into the house from the garden when called. The garden line differs from the house-line, in that it can be about one and a half times as long and is only put on before the dog goes into the garden. When it is time for the dog to come in from the garden, you can make your way to the line, pick it up and teach your dog to go into the house.

Long line

A long line is about 15 metres and is attached to the dog's solid collar enabling it to run free as though off the lead whilst allowing the handler/owner reasonable control and facilitating teaching and training. If your dog does not come when called when out on walks do not let him off the lead without a long line on. At this stage in your dog's training it does not matter if he does not go off the lead to run around. It will help if he gets plenty of mental stimulation through games and play combined with walks on the lead. If at any point he is off his lead and he does not come when you call him, never tell him off for not coming, no matter how long it takes you to entice him to you. He will only associate you calling him with unpleasant consequences and not want to come to you happily. If you are unsure of how he will respond, you can use an extending lead or trailing line. Remember, safety must come first, so take care when using a line.

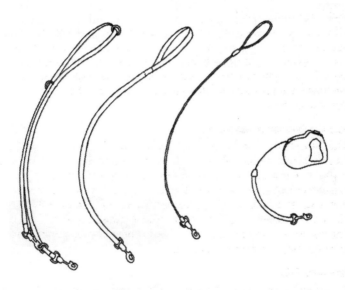

Fig 7 Various speciality leads

Beds

Dogs are by nature denning animals, therefore ideally your dog should have his own place, and an ideal place would be somewhere quiet and warm, such as a utility room, kitchen or hallway. By providing your dog with its own bed you are providing it with its own territory, refuge or reference point.

When considering what type and size to get ensure you allow sufficient space so that your dog is not cramped or that it is not too big.

Types of bed

Dog beds come in a wide variety of shapes and sizes. Ridged plastic types are resilient and suitable generally for most dogs and although they can still be chewed the dog is less likely to chew larger pieces. This type is also easy to clean and a blanket can be placed in the bottom for additional comfort and warmth. The most hygienic blankets for dogs are those made of polyester fur fabric, which are warm and long lasting and easily washed as well as being less appealing to chew unlike woollen blankets. Soft fabrics are popular as they are easily washed simply by putting them through the household washing machine and dogs like to snuggle up in them; smaller breeds tend to like the igloo type, designed for cats, as they can curl up and hide in them. Likewise beanbags are comfortable but can be a bit more difficult to clean. Whilst wicker baskets are traditional they are difficult to clean and pieces that have been chewed can be swallowed which can be dangerous.

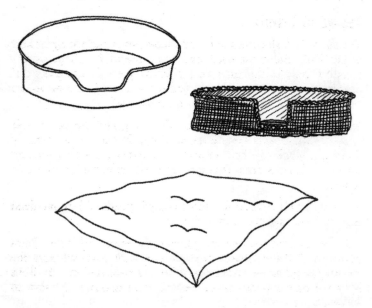

Fig 8 Various beds

Brushes

Keeping your dog's coat clean and free from uncomfortable knots and tangles is obviously more important on longer coated dogs and usually becomes more time consuming as the dog becomes older. If you have a long-coated breed that needs professional trimming or a large breed that you find too time consuming to bathe, or do not have suitable facilities, consider enlisting the services of a professional groomer. Shop around when looking for a salon, a good groomer will be happy to discuss your dog and his needs and will be willing to spend time getting to know your dog. As well as bathing and trimming your dog, a good salon will clean his ears and cut his nails if necessary. Finding a City and Guilds qualified groomer is always a good idea as they will have had to trim various breeds to a high standard to achieve this qualification, as well as taking written exams to prove they have a good general knowledge of dog care.

There are a great variety of products available to assist owners with grooming their dog and by selecting the right brushes and combs for the dog's coat this will undoubtedly save time and help produce the best results.

Types of brush

The slicker brush comes in many shapes, sizes and strengths and is probably the most used and most useful for long, dense-coated breeds. Although a very effective piece of equipment, if used incorrectly it can cause inflammation and irritation to the skin so care should be taken when being used.

Most owners use a pin brush on their dog and the use of this type of brush will benefit most dogs. It acts as a form of massage, which can help improve circulation, muscle tone and promotes healthy skin. It is not, however, effective on knots or tangles.

A bristle brush is ideal for short-coated breeds to remove dead hair and massage the skin and coat.

Palm pads and rubber hound gloves come in several forms. Palm pads are ideal for terriers or dogs with wire coats whereas the rubber hound glove is more suited to short-coated breeds. Both lift dead hair and dirt from the coat and massage the skin to leave a healthy shine.

Moulting combs are available for long- and short-coated dogs and as their name suggests are designed to aid moulting. The long teeth penetrate the under coat to lift dead hair and the shorter teeth collect it.

Fig 9 Various combs and brushes

Food and water bowls

A fresh supply of drinking water is essential for all dogs and a shortage can lead to illness, as it is required for various different functions in the body such as the transportation of blood and elimination of waste.

Each day make up your dog's daily food in the usual way. When you feed your dog, ask him to 'sit', 'give a paw', or anything else you would like your dog to do. In effect your dog is saying 'please'. Allow your dog to eat his food, but once he has walked away from the food bowl, if he has not returned within 10 minutes, pick up the bowl and discard any uneaten food. This portion of food is not re-offered.

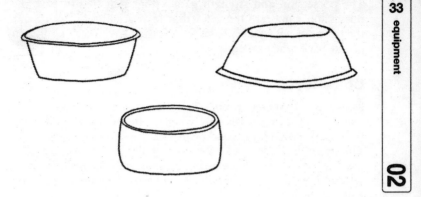

Fig 10 Various bowls

Toys

Dogs enjoy games of strength, possession, kill and chase. The type of games your dog will prefer will depend on what he has been breed for. For example, a Border collie will enjoy chase games, whereas a springer spaniel will enjoy chasing and retrieving. The owner, without knowing, usually encourages their dog to play the wrong games where the dog is learning an inappropriate behaviour, such as games of chase with a ball, but when the article changes to a ten-pound note, the game takes on a new meaning. Therefore, play games where your dog is learning the right behaviour and control the games you play with him.

Games dogs play

The killing game: dogs that play the killing game shake a rag, soft toy or paper from side to side shredding it – but they usually lose interest once it is 'dead'. They also play the killing game with squeaky toys, but again lose all interest after the squeak has been 'killed'. Many dogs will play the killing game to a certain extent, but terriers are the real experts at it.

The chase game: most dogs like to play the 'chase game'. Some dogs are obsessed with this game and want to chase anything that moves. Border collies must be the supreme example of dogs that enjoy the chase game.

The possession and strength game: dogs that like to play the possession game are the ones that love a game of tug-of-war then run off with your possession or their toy and don't like to give it back when asked.

Chew toys

Kongs are a strong rubber toy that are super bouncy and irresistible to dogs, especially when stuffed with treats as they turn into a stimulating food dispenser. Toys that are based on a similar line include food cubers and balls, which are toys that the dog can roll or knock around and having been filled with a selection of treats are gradually dispensed, keeping the dog amused for long periods.

Chew bones might include hard sterilized bones, which are usually either empty or pre filled, such as smoked bones or deep fired barrow bones to softer basted sinew or rawhide chews. Hard rubber toys are available in a variety of colours and assortment of shapes and although they can be destroyed by constant chewing, they provide hours of stimulation and occupation for lots of dogs.

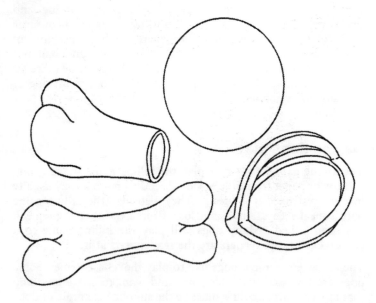

Fig 11 A smoked bone and various other hard, rubber toys

Play toys

Balls or a ball on a rope are perfect for interactive play or teaching retrieve as they can be thrown long distances and come in a variety of sizes and colours.

Many dogs like to carry something in their mouth, especially the gun dog breeds. Rope toys are ideal for such dogs as they are safe and as well as being a toy, provide useful flossing action during interactive play.

Squeaky toys come in a wide variety of shapes and colours and are generally made of rubber or latex, the latter generally lasting a little longer as many dogs love to squeak the toy until they destroy the squeak mechanism and then gradually chew until the toy is unrecognizable.

Other toys may include the more complex ones such as doggy dominoes, rouletter or solitaire. These should only be used under supervision of the owner but are wonderful ways of playing games with your dog.

Fig 12 Simple toys including rope and squeaky toys and complex toys including doggy roulette and solitaire

Indoor kennel/crate

The most popular type of indoor kennel or crate is the fold-down mesh type. They come in a variety of sizes and because they collapse they can be easily transported. The crate is a wonderful training aid if introduced and used correctly.

To introduce the crate correctly, leave the door open and make it comfortable for your puppy. Feed your puppy all his meals in there, and throughout the day toss the odd treat in there for him to go in and get. You will find that he will begin to take himself in there for a nap. Don't just push your puppy in and lock the door on him as this will not make the crate a pleasant place to be.

The crate should be long enough for the dog to turn around in and stretch, also high enough for him to sit up without touching the top. Ideally, the crate should be placed in an area close to the family. Positioning it in a corner, with a sheet or towel covering the top and sides, gives the dog a cosy, secure, 'den' feeling.

A crate can be used when you cannot supervise your puppy, which will mean that your puppy will not get into mischief. A crate can be a big help with housetraining as no dog likes to mess his bed and is likely to cry to be let out to go to the toilet. What it is not is a 'sin bin' where puppies are put for hours at a time.

Do not leave a collar on your puppy when he is alone and in his crate as this can get caught on the bars.

03

socialization

In this chapter you will learn:
- how to understand what socialization is
- how to socialize your puppy effectively
- how to handle and groom your dog effectively.

What is socialization? Socialization is a term that is often misunderstood. It does not mean that a dog is going to learn how to romp and play with other dogs, but rather a term that means habituating or getting a dog used to the environment around it.

Because dogs need to learn and accept the natural world around them and not be scared by things they will come across in their daily lives, they have an inborn period of time called the socialization period. This is a finite time when puppies will be curious and willing to investigate novel things. The time occurs between three and five months, with easy habituation ending about four and a half months depending on breed and personality. You need to expose your puppy to as many things in its environment as possible. If your puppy has not had his vaccinations it is still possible to socialize it. Carry your puppy in your arms so that it can experience the outside world. Ask friends with dogs who are well socialized, have nice temperaments and are fully vaccinated to come round to your house and garden so that your puppy can interact with other dogs.

You puppy's experiences should be positive, using play and treats to form an association with all the things it will encounter throughout his life. These include car rides, the vet's surgery, skateboards, bikes, traffic, children of all ages, men, women, horses; in fact, the list is endless.

cars	men/hat	tarmac	playground	
bikes	men/tall	mud	pensioners	
tractors	men/short	sand	motorbikes	
lorries	women/umbrella	pebbles	bus	
buses	women/tall	lakes	trains	
roads	women/short	the sea	escalators	
vans	women/glasses	prams	markets	
horses/rider	children	pushchairs	fairground	
sheep	bikes	babies		
cows	balls	toddlers		
dogs	skipping	geese		
cats	running	ducks		
men	skateboards	swans		
women	gates	country lane		
children	stiles	busy road		
men/beards	car parks	bridges		
men/glasses	wheelchairs	town centre		
men/umbrella	grass	schools		

Fig 13 Socialization chart – mark in the box how many times your dog has experienced these elements

It is well worth the time and trouble to fit in as many different environmental elements as possible. Make a chart so that you can check how many different things your puppy has encountered.

This chart is just to get you started. The more things you add, the better socialized your dog will be.

You can never cover all eventualities but if you think about it logically, what you are teaching your puppy during this period is to view novel experiences as pleasurable.

Handling your puppy is very important. Your puppy needs to learn that being touched and held is a rewarding experience. Not only will you have to handle your puppy to groom him, dry his feet and maybe take out the odd tic or two but there are many other people that will have to handle your puppy throughout his life. The veterinary surgeon, the groomer and many others. Ask as many people, including children, to handle and hand feed your puppy by sitting on the floor, feeding small tasty treats as they look into his ears, hold onto his paws and feel down his legs and under his tummy.

If your puppy is a shy reserved type, make sure that you allow the interaction to be at his own pace and do not force him to take food. You should always supervise this handling to make sure that your puppy is safe.

Socialization may seem an unnecessary and boring part of your puppy's training but it is critical. The more interesting and pleasurable puppyhood experiences your dog can dip in to in later life, the more resilient and stable its character will be.

Occasionally something can go wrong and your puppy will view the experience as frightening. Whatever the bad experience, it must be addressed sensibly and unemotionally. You need to re-establish that the element is safe and pleasant.

One of the more common problems encountered is when another dog or puppy is overly aggressive. If your puppy has been frightened by the encounter it is imperative that he is introduced to gentle, safe and sociable dogs as soon after his frightening experience as possible. Your puppy should be allowed to interact with this type of dog at his own pace, allowing him to learn that other dogs are not threatening. If you are unsure about finding the right type of dog to reintroduce your puppy to contact your local APDT trainer and ask if they can help.

Puppy classes

Choose your puppy class carefully!

A qualified and knowledgeable trainer should supervise any puppy-to-puppy play. They will understand the importance of having puppies of similar temperament playing together and what harm can be done if some simple order is not adhered to!

All training in a good puppy class should use positive reinforcement. This means teaching your puppy by rewarding the behaviour you like, rather than punishing the behaviour you do not like.

All APDT trainers use positive reinforcement methods and can easily be contacted by going to the website **www.apdt.co.uk** or contacting your local vet who will have a directory with all APDT members listed.

The older puppy or dog

If you have taken on an older dog this does not mean it cannot be socialized. It just takes longer and sometimes you may find that the dog has already built up some bad associations. As with a puppy, introduce your dog to as many environmental elements as possible associating each one with a rewarding experience.

Note: If your dog is showing any fearful, worried or aggressive behaviour, contact a professional dog behaviourist. This behaviour can be addressed but needs a specialized plan of action for the individual dog.

Dog-to-dog socialization

Under-socialized dogs will not necessarily be fearful around other dogs. They may well be interested in other dogs but just lack social greeting skills. Many puppy or adolescent dogs are way over the top when greeting other dogs and can annoy older dogs with their crude and often boisterous body language.

The best way of teaching these dogs how to interact with their own kind is to give them regular contact with *well-socialized* adult dogs. These dogs will not tolerate too much crude behaviour but will do no harm when showing the younger dog how to behave. The very worst you can do with these young under-skilled dogs is to keep them away from other dogs. If they are not allowed to learn the correct greeting manoeuvres valuable social lessons will never be learnt. Training during this period is crucial. We all want dogs that socialize well with their own species but not at the expense of ignoring their owners. Dogs and puppies need to learn how to walk past another dog without interacting with it.

- With your dog on a flat collar and lead ask him to sit as another dog approaches.
- Keep a reasonable distance between the two dogs and reward your dog as he sits and the other dog walks past.
- Be generous with your rewards at this stage and keep your dog's attention on you. As long as your dog remains in a sit, reward with small tasty treats.
- Use the same technique to teach your dog to walk politely past another dog.
- As the unknown dog approaches have a handful of small rewards ready and attract your dog's attention by saying his name and a command to 'look'.
- When your dog pays attention to you give a reward.
- Keep doing this as the other dog walks past.

If you think about this from your dog's point of view you are teaching him the habit of automatically looking to you when another dog approaches. As the habit of training becomes ingrained you can reward your dog at less frequent intervals. There will be times when you will allow your dog to interact with other dogs but using this technique you will have a dog that will look to you for permission to interact with a strange dog. Teach your dog that there are different signals or cues when another dog approaches.

- The signal of look or listen means pay attention to you and ignore the other dog.
- The signal of 'say hello' or something similar means you can interact with the other dog.

When your dog is off lead and playing with another dog you will need to know how to regain his attention.

Read the section in Chapter 06 on recall training.

Handling and grooming

All dogs must learn how to cope with being handled. This may be for grooming purposes, for veterinary treatment or simply being petted. Some dogs love being touched and will actively crave attention by pushing their muzzle under a hand or pawing at you. Others dislike or are indifferent about physical contact. This does not make one type of dog better than the other, just different! Learning to enjoy human handling is imperative and your reward for taking the time and trouble to teach your dog these lessons will be a dog that other people find a pleasure.

The best way to teach your dog how to enjoy being handled is to associate handling with something pleasant.

Whether your dog is long- or short-coated they all need to be brushed. Not only will this keep your dog's coat and skin in good condition but will also help you spot any abnormalities such as lumps or skin irritations.

Most dogs find different parts of their body more sensitive than others. With some it may be the tail, others behind the ears or maybe their paws. If your dog shows a dislike of having a particular part of his body being touched do not avoid this area, rather pay special attention to associating this with a rewarding experience. This is especially important around the tail region, as that is where the vet will put a thermometer if your dog needs to have his temperature taken.

Introducing stages of grooming

Before we start let's think about what we want the dog to learn?

We want the dog not just to tolerate grooming but actually enjoy the experience. The easiest way to teach this is to exploit the way a dog learns.

Dogs spend their time watching for signals that will affect their lives. A signal can mean something good is going to happen or something bad.

A lead usually signals a good thing is going to happen, a walk!
A tin opener signals dinner!
A hand signals food or toys!

A brush can signal a bad thing is about to happen, having your fur pulled. Nail clippers can signal restraint and if done badly pain! Hands can signal punishment or maybe denial of something.

We need to teach the dog that hands, brushes, nail clippers and so on are signals that something good is going to happen.

Introducing grooming signals

Run your hand gently along your dog's body and then give your dog a tasty titbit. Teach your dog that every time your hand appears and touches him it is a signal that something good is going to happen. Repeat this until your dog is showing you he is looking forward to being touched. Your aim is for your dog to enjoy being touched all over. As I mentioned at the beginning some dogs will find this an easy exercise and others may take a little longer. When your dog is happy being handled it is time to introduce a brush.

Produce the brush and then give your dog a titbit. Repeat this until your dog is obviously enjoying the brush appearing. Move on to touching your dog with the brush and then feeding a very tasty titbit. When your dog is actively showing you that being touched by the brush is something he is looking forward to go on to the next stage of actually brushing your dog. Start with short sessions, perhaps brushing different parts of your dog at each session. Remember to give your dog an interesting titbit each time you brush him. Using the same technique:

1 Check his paws and between the toes. Dogs will often pick up grass seeds and these must be removed.

2 When your dog is happy to have his paws held, introduce the nail clippers. Do this in exactly the same way using the clippers to signal something good is going to happen.

3 Space this over as many sessions as is necessary for your dog to feel happy when the clippers are produced. Move on to touching your dog's claws with the clippers.

4 When your dog is responding in a way that tells you he likes the clippers to touch his nails cut just one nail per session using the same signalling technique. Never cut below the quick, as just like us this is very painful and will bleed profusely.

5 Teeth must be kept clean and checked often. This is done by giving your dog a word or cue such as 'open', opening his mouth gently and popping in a food treat. Your dog should soon learn to associate the word 'open' with opening his mouth.

6 To clean your dog's teeth, take a small amount of *dog toothpaste*, place it on your finger and rub it around the gums and teeth. After a few sessions of this you can progress to a small-headed toothbrush and gently brush your dog's teeth.

7 If you keep up with this routine two or three times a week throughout your dog's life you will keep your dog's teeth healthy, therefore prolonging his life.

8 Ears and eyes need to be kept free of foreign bodies, so you need to teach your dog to enjoy having these checked. Ears should have a pleasant odour. If your dog's ears have an unpleasant smell it is an indication that he has an infection and must be taken to the vet immediately.

Your dog may show signs of not wishing to have parts of his body handled. This can take the form of keeping very still and growling or perhaps wriggling and biting. *Never* punish your dog for displaying this type of behaviour. He is using the only way he knows to tell you not to touch this area. Take your dog to the vet and make sure that he is physically well. If your dog is fit and well but still displaying these signs it is because past experience has taught him that growling or biting has the desired effect, e.g. humans back away. Contact your nearest member of the APDT who will either help you sort the problem out without punishment or will be able to refer you to the nearest qualified behaviour counsellor, and they will help you understand and correct the undesired behaviour.

Remember, grooming and handling your dog should be a pleasant experience for both of you.

04

before you begin

In this chapter you will learn:
- how to decide what you want from your dog
- about the right words to use
- how to get the family on track.

Taking on a puppy is a big responsibility. He may be a member of your family for the next 14 or 15 years, so you need to start the way you mean to carry on. There are two key points to consider before training begins or even before you get your puppy.

1 What you want or don't want your adult dog to do in the house.

2 What you want or don't want your adult dog to do in the way of obedience inside or outside.

Indoors

Chapter 05 looks at 'Puppy issues' and explains how to train your dog to be a well-behaved member of your family while in the house. Therefore, the first thing you must do as a family is to decide what will be acceptable for your dog to do indoors and what won't.

Before you get your puppy, sit down as a family and write a list of things that you are happy for your puppy to do indoors and those that you will not be quite so happy with. Then, beside each of those items write a command word, or 'cue' word, that you will use when teaching your puppy for each of those items. When using 'cue' words, the entire family must be consistent in their use. If someone in the family uses a different word, then it will only confuse your puppy and make the training process longer. For example, the first thing you are likely to teach a puppy is to eliminate outside so you will need a 'cue' word, but it must be consistent if your puppy is to learn to eliminate outside in the shortest possible time. As he becomes more accustomed to eliminating outside, the 'cue' word can be used to let your pup know what you are expecting of him.

Alternatively you may not want your adult dog lying on your sofa, so firstly do not encourage him onto the sofa when he is still a pup, or if you would like him on the sofa sometimes but not others you still need to teach a 'cue' to invite him up and another 'cue' to ask him to get off.

You may not want your puppy to go into certain rooms, the baby's bedroom for example. Baby gates are really useful to block off rooms where your dog is not allowed without having to shut him out altogether. So purchase your baby gates before your puppy arrives home so you start as you mean to go on.

Having decided on your list and 'cue' words, write them down and attach them to the fridge door with fridge magnets so if at any time someone forgets what a 'cue' word is, they can easily refer to it.

Outdoors

Similarly, you will need to decide as a family what you would like your dog to do in the way of basic obedience. Chapter 06 describes a number of things that most pet dog owners would like their dog to do, but just as teaching what is and isn't acceptable indoors, your dog will need to be taught a 'cue' word for each obedience exercise. Depending on your experiences with dogs, you might find teaching the right exercises to have a well-behaved sociable dog is sufficient. On the other hand, if you are a more experienced owner you might like to be a little more adventurous and teach more advanced exercises. Whatever you require from your dog, decide on a 'cue' word for each exercise; write a list of each exercise and write the 'cue' word next to it so everyone in the family uses the same word for the same exercise.

Once you have a list of what you want to teach your puppy and the 'cue' words for each exercise, then attach them to the fridge door.

A word about words

It's important to think about the words you will be using as 'cue' words so as not to confuse your puppy.

One of the first things your puppy will need to learn is his name. When to use his name and when not to use his name is very important. Primarily you should use your puppy's name to get his attention. Once you have his attention you can then give him a command, or 'cue', and while you have his attention, you needn't repeat it every time you give a command. For example, if you want your puppy to do a sequence of sit, stay, come to you, and sit, you would say his name initially to get his attention, then the 'cues' for each exercise individually. A common mistake is to go through this sequence by saying. 'Rover sit; Rover stay; Rover come; Rover sit.' What you will end up with is words where the puppy's name and the 'cue' word join together and end up as 'roversit, roverstay, rovercome, roversit' and your puppy's name will eventually become meaningless.

Also avoid using your puppy's name as a 'cue' to call him back to you. Your puppy will hear his name mentioned probably dozens of times a day. You will use it to get his attention; you'll probably talk to him and use his name, 'good boy, Rover' for example. You may have conversations with friends or neighbours where his name is mentioned; he may not react but he will hear it. For this reason, it can be very confusing for your puppy to know whether he is needed to do something or not whenever he hears his name.

Words that sound the same but have different meanings can be confusing. For example, if you use the word 'heel' to teach your puppy to walk nicely beside you on the lead and the word 'here' to get him to come back to you, the two words sound similar and can therefore confuse your puppy. So try to think of words that are very clear and dissimilar.

It's very easy to use human terminology on our dogs and expect them to understand. How many times is the term 'sit down' used to get people, well, to sit down? It's very common to use the word 'sit' to teach a puppy to sit, and 'down' to get him to lie down. If you use these words for those exercises, then saying, 'sit down' to your puppy is only going to confuse him. 'Do they want me to sit or lie down?' So use 'sit' for sit and 'down' for down. Alternatively, if you want to use 'sit down' when teaching your puppy to sit, you will need to think of another 'cue' to teach him to lie down, 'flat' for example.

It's also very easy but unwise to use a word that means several different actions. The word 'down' is a good example. 'Down' can mean 'lie down', 'get off the furniture', and 'stop jumping up at me'. That is one word for three different actions. When making your list of what you want to teach your puppy, whether indoors or outdoors, think of 'cues' that are unique to a particular exercise or command so you have one word meaning one thing.

Motivation

You are also going to have to find out what motivates your puppy. With many dogs, particularly puppies, food is a great motivator but you will need to find out *what* food motivates him more than anything else. You will need to find several different foods and grade them as to how much he values them. A piece of dry kibble that he is fed for his meals three or four times a day may motivate him but only for so long. A piece of frankfurter on the other hand may be a jackpot motivator! You will need to grade the rewards as the training progresses, so once you have found several foods that motivate your puppy, use the lower grade first and when he's doing really well, you can use the jackpot motivator. Keep a regular check on your puppy's weight during the early training and make adjustments to his daily food intake if necessary.

Other pups are motivated by toys but again you must find several toys that will motivate him and grade them so you start with a low grade toy and know what his jackpot toy is when he's done really well.

You may find that as you progress with training, some things will motivate your puppy indoors while others will be more motivating outdoors. Food is usually associated with indoor activities as that's where your puppy is fed. Outdoors is where you play with your puppy more vigorously than indoors, so toys may be more motivating outdoors. It's just a question of experimenting and finding out what *your puppy* really likes rather than what *you* want him to like.

Older dogs

If you acquire an older dog from a re-homing centre, you may be fortunate that he may be trained to a certain degree. In which case the re-homing staff should be able to provide you with a list of commands the dog understands. Do not change these commands unless there is a very good reason. If you change the commands for no reason, this will only confuse the dog and you will virtually be re-training him.

If your new dog is not trained then you will have to start from scratch as with a puppy (described above). There is a risk, however, that if your dog has not been trained he may very well have some 'bad habits', so these will have to be sorted out while you are training your dog. The principle of thinking about what you want your dog to do, or not to do, being consistent with the commands and finding out what motivates him are the same as with a puppy. For more information about re-homed dogs, please refer to Chapter 14, 'Taking it further'.

05
puppy issues

In this chapter you will learn:
- how to house train your puppy
- how to deal with 'puppy biting'
- how to prevent problem behaviours.

The importance of play

Puppies need to learn how to relate to their own species, how to read body signals, how to use body language to deflect aggressive displays, how to invite play with other dogs, how to build a relationship with us as their owners and they do all this through play.

Through playing with other dogs and puppies they learn the importance of having a soft mouth, effective use of body language and how to deal with dogs of all shapes and sizes. Through playing with his owner he will learn the basis of a good relationship, all manner of cues, how to have self control, how to wait for something he wants, and most importantly of all how to have fun with us.

It is sad to see some dogs walking around the park doing their own thing while their owner is chatting to other dog owners, only to call the dog back at the end of the walk and put him back on the lead. The dog is usually out of control and with little in the way of training and a poor relationship with his owner. If you spend time playing games with your puppy you will teach him you are a great deal more fun than every other dog and person in the park.

Play can help build the confidence of a shy dog and can teach a boisterous dog calm if you teach him how to wait for what he wants.

Appropriate games

There are many games that we can play with our puppy and as owners we should actively encourage and enjoy them, but some games are wholly inappropriate and can lead to a great deal of trouble when your puppy becomes a fully grown dog. Rough and tumble games are a great favorite, especially with the men in the house and children when your puppy is small, but these kind of games will quickly escalate out of control, and you could be heading for disaster. Play games that you can all play together. Hide and seek around the garden can also help with recalls, hold onto your puppy and send one of the children to go and hide then get the puppy go find, as soon as puppy gets there give him a treat; fetch, but please make sure that the balls that you play with are a suitable size for your puppy, too small and they may choke him; playing with a tuggie and, of course, the best games of all are training games. When puppies and children work together training they build a better and trusting relationship. If your training is fun for you it will certainly be fun for your puppy. If you have a shy puppy you may scare him if you try to play a chasing game with him. Turn it the other way around and try and encourage him to chase you instead. He may, with time, build his confidence enough to be chased back making it a two-way game. Put a cue on this so your dog knows what is coming as you get in position for a great game of chase. If you have children you really do need to supervise this game or not let them play with your puppy in this way. Care should always be at the forefront of your thinking about suitability of certain games with certain breeds of dogs. Chasing games with a Border collie and children could be asking for trouble and rough games with one of the bull breeds can quickly get out of control.

House-training

It will depend on how vigilant you are as to how long it will take to house-train your puppy. It can also depend on his size, as larger dogs tend to be quicker to house-train – they have larger bladders and so can hold on to their urine longer through the night. It will also depend on what you have heard from your breeder on how house-training has been started, if at all. It can also depend on the diet that you feed. If you feed a dried diet your dog will need to drink more and so urinate more; if you feed a cheaper diet that has bulk added there is more waste and your dog will want to poo more.

Many people still use newspaper in the house to house-train their puppy, but what you are doing is environmentally training your puppy that it is OK to go inside the house and now you have to change this and teach him you actually would like him to go to the toilet outside. So house-training can take double the amount of time. If you do use newspaper, how will he know the difference between the newspaper you have put in the kitchen and the paper you put on the floor near the sofa that you hadn't finished reading yet?

Most puppies give many clues that they are just about to 'go', they may sniff the floor and circle, they may become agitated and move around while they are looking for somewhere to go, they may whine or they move towards the door and you may miss it, only finding the puddle on the floor later on.

Puppies will usually, but nothing is set in stone, go on waking, not long after they have eaten and after a good play time. Take your puppy outside and let him wander around and sniff, don't play with him or talk to him, you just want him to sniff the ground and go to the toilet, you don't want to distract him from the job in hand. Let him begin to go to the toilet before you say 'good boy' as he may stop what he is doing and come to you. When he has finished going to the toilet reward him with a small titbit. Don't take him inside to give him a titbit for going to the toilet outside as you will be rewarding him for going back into the house – take a small treat with you outside and reward him as soon as he has finished. Puppies are very food motivated and you will find your house training will be a great deal quicker if you reward him every time he goes to the toilet outside.

If your puppy has an accident inside the house and you don't see him just clean it up with cleaner specifically for the job (available from your local pet shop). If you use household disinfectant or bleach it will only mask the smell from your nose for a short while. Your puppy has a much better sense of smell than you have and will sniff around the carpet, and smelling old urine and ammonia will stimulate him to go on that spot again. If you do catch him in the middle of going to the toilet inside the house, make a loud noise to distract him and take him outside as quickly as possible, the noise to distract him may be you clapping your hands, shouting 'oi!' or banging on the door. Don't punish him or you will teach him that going to the toilet when you are around is not nice and so even if you are outside he will not want to go to the toilet while you are there. House-training takes time and consistency, if you need to leave your dog for a good deal of time try and get a member of the family or a neighbour to call in and let him out to go to the toilet.

Play biting

Puppy owners often get worried that they have an aggressive puppy when their puppies are jumping up biting them. This is natural behaviour for a puppy, this is how they would play with their litter mates and this is when they would learn just how hard they shouldn't bite! When your puppy arrives at your home he has no more litter mates to play with and so he will play with you and the way puppies play is using their teeth. Puppies will also bite a bit more when they begin to lose their puppy teeth, and it is important that they are given something suitable to chew and relieve their teeth and gums. Puppy teeth are needle sharp and can be very painful. There are lots of puppy toys that you can give them to keep them busy but do be careful as the soft plastic toys are easily chewed to pieces in a matter of minutes. Whenever you give your puppy a new toy watch him with it for a couple of minutes to make sure that it can withstand your puppy's teeth. Rope raggy toys are something that they can get their teeth into, you could also freeze a carrot and give that to your puppy to chew, the coldness should ease his gums if they are sore from teething. Cardboard boxes are good as a disposable toy, yes it makes a mess but it's better than the mess your puppy could make of the furniture, and boxes can be replaced easily. If you do use cardboard boxes make sure that any staples are removed first. You can fill a small cardboard box with scrunched up newspaper and hide biscuits for him to have some fun and keep his teeth off your skin for a while. Puppies do usually grow out of play biting by the time they are about twenty weeks but it is an important lesson your puppy learns from you while he is still using his teeth.

Bite inhibition

Teaching bite inhibition is all about teaching your puppy just how hard his bite is and teaching him to have a soft mouth. It teaches your puppy how to use his mouth gently. Accidents happen, your child might ride over your dog's tail with his bike, you may come home drunk on New Year's Day and fall over your dog. If you hurt your dog he only has one defence, his mouth. If he ever gets in the position where he feels he has to bite and he has good bite inhibition then damage will be minimal. Every dog can bite. If frightened enough or in pain or threatened, your dog 'will' bite. That doesn't in any way make him a 'bad' dog. It makes him a dog! It is your responsibility therefore to teach your dog that human skin is incredibly fragile. If you teach your dog bite inhibition, that training will carry over even if he is later in a position where he feels he has no other option but to bite.

Teaching bite inhibition is in four stages. The first two stages are all about making the bites softer, and the second two stages are about decreasing the frequency of bites. The training must be done in this order because if you decrease the frequency first your dog won't learn to soften his bite.

- No painful bites. 90 per cent of puppies will stop biting you if you give a loud high-pitched yelp. If your puppy backs off, praise and reinforce by continuing your game. The other 10 per cent of puppies who just bite harder and get more excited by your loud high-pitched yelp are usually over tired, over stimulated or belong to the terrier breeds. If this is your puppy then you need to end the game as soon as your puppy begins to bite – get up and walk away. It does not require any punishment at all; your puppy is just being a puppy.

- If you end the game you need to get away from your puppy with as little fuss or attention as possible. Even negative attention is attention. It is often helpful to have your puppy on a house-line, so you can move him out of the way when he begins to bite too hard. Or, have a baby gate up so you can move yourself totally out of the area. Because the getting up and moving is tough to do at the instant the undesired behaviour occurs, consider using a hand signal or word that will always mean 'fun's over'. Use it consistently when your puppy is showing you behaviour you would rather not have, you are going to withdraw attention and the behaviour should decrease, as you are no longer acknowledging it. Puppy teeth do hurt and can make you bleed but you do need to have patience with this, puppy mouthing is 100 per cent natural behaviour, it's not meanness, it's a puppy being a puppy.

- You now need to teach your puppy to use less pressure. Basically you do this gradually. Set a limit on how hard your dog can bite. If he bites harder, yelp. Gradually set your limit softer and softer. Remember to do this gradually. A big jump in this is confusing and frustrating for your puppy. And you need to be very clear to him on exactly what you want.

- When you say 'stop', your puppy stops! Teach him 'take it' and 'leave it' (see the training exercises in Chapter 06). You need to be able to start and stop the game instantly.

- Your puppy may never touch a human with his mouth unless invited. Basically this is just taking all this and having it all under cue.

None of these stages require anything more punishing than time outs or withdrawal of attention. When teaching these behaviours put your hands in your dog's mouth all the time. Get him used to your being there. Make sure you can open his mouth and examine his teeth, the vet is going to do it, and you should prepare your puppy for it.

Chewing

Puppies chew for various reasons, boredom, teething, exploring things with their mouth and it is up to us to teach them what is acceptable to chew and what is not. All puppies chew as they begin to lose their teeth at around the age of four months. They begin another teething stage when they reach around eight months as their teeth set into their jaw. Both stages are a necessary part of puppy development and some breeds of dog excel at chewing. A dog will not know the difference between a dining chair and a lump of wood in the garden, it's all chew sticks to him.

As an owner you have to redirect his chewing to acceptable items. Provide plenty of 'safe' chewing toys. Kongs are excellent and practically indestructible. Soft plastic toys can be dangerous and are chewed to bits in minutes. Roasted bones can be bought from pet shops, but ensure there are no loose splinted bits of bone before giving to your puppy. These can be refilled again and again to keep your puppy busy for hours. Kongs and bones can be filled with many different things so your dog need never get bored with these – cream cheese, part of his dinner, marmite, and anything else you can think of.

A stuffed Kong is excellent to guard against chewing if you have to leave him alone for a period of time. It will keep him occupied and tire him out a little. If you do catch your puppy chewing an inappropriate item, distract him and then give him something he *can* chew.

Jumping up

Jumping up begins when we bring our puppy home, they reach up to get as near to us as possible for greeting and when they are small and cute we tend to encourage this behaviour by bending down to stroke them. While this is cute, by the time your dog is 8–9 months old and nearly fully grown it is a different story and a fully-grown labrador jumping up is downright dangerous.

Jumping up is one of those behaviours that is quickly learnt as a puppy as being a rewarding pastime and is something that is certainly rewarded by the attention it receives, but it is one of the hardest habits to break in an older dog. The secret of breaking the habit is not letting it start in the first place.

Puppies jump to get attention, and they get it in three ways, by touch, sight and sound. An owner pushing a puppy down is reward enough – touch, then the owner begins saying 'no, off' – sound, and an owner might look at the puppy – sight. All things a puppy wants.

To avoid rewarding this behaviour, get down to your puppy's level when you first greet him so he will not have to jump up to get your attention. When he has all feet on the floor reward him with what he wants, your attention. When he does jump up, ignore him by not looking at him as some dogs find this rewarding in itself, and not pushing him off you, fold your arms and turn yourself away from him. Have patience with this and when he tires of jumping, and stands there with four feet on the floor, praise, praise, praise. Dogs learn by what gets rewarded – rewarding for them that is, and it is vital that you are extremely consistent in rewarding the behaviour you want. It is also vital that you do not let your children or visitors encourage this behaviour, many visitors say that it is OK that your puppy is jumping because 'they love dogs' but this is unfair to the dog. It is not OK that your puppy jumps up on any visitors so be very strict that visitors do not reinforce the behaviour that you do not want.

Prevention of food guarding

Food guarding is a natural behaviour for a dog to display but is scary for owners to witness and rewarding for the dog as he growls and owners back off perplexed by their dog's behaviour. In that instant the dog learns that his behaviour has worked. As owners we tend to miss the first signals our dog gives that he is unhappy with anyone around his food dish. He may freeze slightly, he may watch you out of the corner of his eye to see how near to his food dish you will get. When we have missed these first signals that he has given that he is unhappy with someone around him he then escalates this to maybe a low growl. If you ignore that warning he may well bite. Your puppy may have learnt to food guard when still with his litter mates, if the breeder fed all the puppies out of the same dish, then he may have had to push and shove to get his share. Food becomes a valuable resource to your puppy. Never punish or shout at your puppy when he gives you that first warning growl – teach him nice things are going to happen when you are around his food bowl.

It used to be said that owners should take their puppy's food bowl away, but this is the quickest and easiest way to teach your puppy how to have a food-guarding problem. There are various ways to teach your puppy to be happy with both children and adults around when he is eating his meal.

When you first get your puppy home stay with him when you feed him, carry on as normal, as you walk past your puppy while he is eating toss in something extra special, say a piece of cheese, or a piece of chicken. Make him look forward to you being around him.

High value resources could also have the same effect on your puppy. Stolen socks, hide chews, bones, etc. Anything that your puppy sees as valuable in his eyes he may be inclined to guard. Training your puppy to give things up on cue is an important part of your training with your puppy (see Chapter 11).

Household etiquette

By invitation only

If you do not want your puppy on the furniture when he is a fully-grown dog, then do not let him on the furniture when he is a puppy. It's very easy when he is small and cute to have him on the furniture for a cuddle when he is tired and children usually like the puppy to be up on the sofa with them to watch the TV. Problems arise when your puppy gets bigger and begins to take up more of the sofa, or he comes in from a good run in the park, he is nice and muddy and is now ready for a rest on the sofa, which is the last place that you want him to be at that moment.

Make sure that he has a nice comfortable bed of his own in your lounge. Some breeds of dog are not comfortable lying on the floor and like something comfortable to lie on. If you want a cuddle from your puppy sit on the floor with him.

If you want to invite your puppy on to the sofa then that is fine, it would be a good idea to teach your puppy to get 'on' and 'off' on cue so that you can move him when you want. When your puppy is on the sofa get a small titbit in your hand, lure your puppy off the sofa, as he is getting off put the cue on the behaviour, then repeat the process when getting the puppy 'on'. Practise a number of times a day, working up to asking the puppy to get 'on' and 'off' without a lure but reward afterwards.

Problems can start by owners getting worked up when the puppy jumps on the sofa and so they grab their puppy by the collar to get him off, the puppy gets a fright and growls at the owner. This can then escalate until the problem is out of control. Don't use threats or force to get your dog off the sofa, if he guards the sofa as a comfortable rescource then distract him by knocking on the front door and then block his access to that room for now and work on teaching him cues if you do want to allow him on the sofa.

Restricted access

It is wise not to let your puppy follow you around the house all the time, he may become too dependent on you being there and when the time comes for you to have to leave him alone he may become very distressed, barking, whining and chewing. Use baby gates strategically around the house so he cannot have access to you all the time. When he is tired, say after a game and a walk, leave him in the kitchen alone in his bed while you get on with other things. He may whine and bark for your attention to begin with, but if you know he does not want to go to the toilet then ignore his whining as he will learn he only has to bark and whine for you to come running. If he does whine then go out of the room for a few seconds and wait for quiet, count to ten and then go back to the puppy while he is still quiet. When he is happy with that much make the time you are out of the room longer and longer. You can leave your puppy with a stuffed Kong so that he is being self-rewarded for being alone. You are going to have to leave your puppy alone at sometime in his life so if you get the work done early on it will make your life much easier when he is older.

Table manners

It is wise not to feed your dog from the table as there is nothing like a dog nudging and whining, waiting for you to give him a titbit. Children are great at teaching puppies how to beg at tables, they don't like what is on their plate so they slip it to the dog under the table! If you do not begin this habit then your puppy is never rewarded for it. If you use a puppy crate you can pop him in the crate with a stuffed Kong or hide chew so he is self-rewarded for lying quietly and not begging at the table, explain to your children why they should not feed the puppy from their plates. If you don't have a crate put your puppy's bed in a quiet corner and leave him there with his Kong.

Manners with food (telling to sit and/or wait before allowing him to eat)

Teaching your puppy to sit and wait for his food is all about teaching him self-control, if he can control himself enough to wait for his meal it is the beginning of teaching him control in a wide variety of situations; when other dogs are around, when there are lots of visitors, in any situation you want him to sit and wait for something. It is all about teaching him manners and if you wait for eye contact you can teach your puppy to look at you first if he wants something.

Get your puppy's dish and ask for a sit, put your finger under his collar and push the dish a little distance away from you. Wait until your puppy relaxes back into a sit and then release him with a cue of your choice, 'go get it'. As meal times go by it should get quicker and quicker for your dog to relax into a sit before he eats. When he is sitting and waiting without any help from you, you can then wait until your puppy makes eye contact before you allow him to eat. This will reiterate him looking to you when he wants to do something.

Building confidence

If your puppy is a shy puppy then you will need to teach him to be confident with the world around him. Socializing him may be slower than your average puppy and will need to go at a pace that he can cope with without overwhelming him. Building confidence can begin in the home, the shy puppy will want to follow you everywhere around the home, including the bathroom and the toilet. Teaching your dog to be alone for a couple of minutes in another room will be the first steps to getting him used to being alone. It is important that you do not let him follow you constantly around the house, the use of baby gates can be of great help here. Leave him behind the baby gate for a moment and go back to him before he has a chance to start barking for you, then praise him. Take your time but add time on to this until he is happy while you are busy doing housework, etc. If your puppy does bark, and you know that it is you he is barking for and not to go out to the toilet then ignore this, when he pauses for breath, go back to him and praise him for his quiet moment. His quiet moments should get longer. This can take time depending on the individual temperament of the dog but will pay dividends later on when you need to leave him alone.

If your puppy is shy of other dogs and people then it is imperative that you get him in to a good puppy class as soon as possible with a trainer who will understand that he needs gentle, careful socializing. Watch a puppy class first to make sure it is not a free for all, where all the puppies are running around causing havoc and learning to bully and be bullied. It is important that you do not force your puppy into situations that he cannot deal with and expect him to get used to it, as he may not and a traumatic event can have far-reaching consequences that only become evident when he is that bit older. Try and ignore fearful behaviour but be there to take your puppy out of a situation he is not happy with, there is nothing wrong with taking him away from something that is just to much for his temperament. But remember what it was and work on teaching him that whatever it was that scared him is rewarded by playing games or feeding him really special treats when the scary thing is around. Heavily praise any brave behaviour that he shows. If you reward the right behaviour and try and ignore the nervous behaviour his confidence should come on in leaps and bounds.

06

training

In this chapter you will learn:
- how to teach your dog to respond first time to his name
- how to teach your dog to sit on cue
- how to teach your dog to come when called.

Rewards and treats

Rewards and treats come in all different shapes, sizes, tastes and smells.

If you go into any pet shop, big or small, on the shelves you will find an interesting array of things we humans call dog treats. These can be very useful and convenient but beware! Just like human junk food some of these products are over-processed and full of colourings and preservatives.

It is very quick and simple to make your own dog treats. Below are some ideas for treats that can be made in just a few minutes. (See Chapter 13 for further recipes for dogs.)

If you are using food rewards to train your dog here are a few tips:

- Use small pieces that are easily and quickly chewed and swallowed.
- When working outdoors it is often more difficult to get your dog's attention. Use food that has a strong smell, garlic sausage or Edam cheese is often considered irresistible by our canine friends.
- Liver, chicken and turkey can be cooked quickly and easily in the microwave.
- Do not always use the same rewards. Just like us, dogs like to have a change; the same old treat becomes boring and therefore non-rewarding.
- Some dogs enjoy raw vegetables and fruit such as carrots or pieces of apple.

There are toys such as the Kong that can be packed with food to keep your dog occupied.

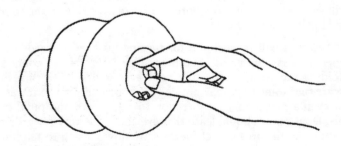

Fig 14 A Kong being filled

a Kong:

Kong with something soft; fish or meat paste,
, pâté or something similar.

thing crunchy, such as dog biscuits and carrot into
, this will take the dog longer to remove.

all fill the spaces with small tasty pieces of food such
cken or sausage.

Who me?

When you use your dog's name he should look at you expectantly, not completely ignore you and be oblivious to what you would like him to do. He should also not slink away into the corner or keep out of sight! If you build up a good association with your dog's name you will improve your relationship with him and find he is really keen to listen to you and respond with a wagging tail.

Your aim is to get your dog to look at you the first time you say his name and then you can follow it through with the cue of what you want him to do; 'sit and watch me', 'leave it' or 'come here' for instance. But first of all you need to teach him to respond to his name.

Begin in a place where there are no distractions, inside the house is a good idea. Have your dog on the lead and call his name in an excited tone of voice when he is looking away from you. The second he turns his head towards you praise him immediately and reward him with a treat. It is important that you do not repeat his name if he ignores you as you will want him to respond to you the first time you call his name, it could be a matter of safety! Clap your hands to get his attention or take a step backwards in order to get his attention. Repeating his name will simply teach him to ignore you or answer you on the third or fourth time you say it.

At first you will reward him for turning his head towards you when you say his name. The next stage is to get eye contact. Holding the treat up towards your eyes will achieve this. Be aware that some dogs may not like eye contact at first so reward for even a glance in your direction to begin with and build on this. Dogs really should learn that eye contact is very rewarding and not at all threatening! Never stare down a dog to tell him off, it is an old-fashioned theory in dog training that has no place in dog training today!

Progress to holding eye contact for a few seconds after you have used his name, and then reward him. Build this up so that you can maintain eye contact for about one minute.

It is important to start this exercise where there are no distractions, and then begin to introduce them gradually. When he is good in the house, and in every room, then take your training into the garden, when he is responsive in the garden and he will come away from what he is doing, you are ready to take your training out on the road so to speak! When you first begin this in the park, again begin when there are no distractions. You may well have to take your training back a step and raise the value of the reward when you begin with really hard distractions, such as other dogs being present!

Do try very hard not to use his name as a reprimand or to nag him, or to call him to you to carry out something that he sees as unpleasant, i.e. cutting his nails, giving him a bath, giving him a worming tablet. Go and get him in those scenarios. Children can sometimes be guilty of saying their dog's name over and over again, and if you have a few children the sound of his name just becomes background noise to your dog. To get over this get your children involved with the training and explain to them the importance of teaching your dog to respond to his name the first time you call him.

Once your dog understands that his name means 'look at me and something good will happen' you can use his name when he is off lead but only a few feet away from you. Don't forget to reward him instantly for turning to look at you.

This exercise is also invaluable in circumstances when you need your dog to sit calmly and look at you. Use it at any time you do not want you dog to interact with other people or dogs. All dogs need to learn self-control and you can teach this by getting a good response to his name followed by eye contact. However friendly your dog is he should not lunge towards other dogs and/or people when walking on the lead. Just training him to respond to his name and sit quietly and watch you will teach him to behave calmly around distractions and defer to you rather than make his own choices.

If your dog already has a history of ignoring you when you call his name, you will have to work extra hard at this exercise. There can be a number of reasons why dogs ignore you, the most common being we have over used their name without following it up with a command; this usually happens in the park when owners only call the dog's name and expect the dog to understand it means 'I would like you to come here now please!' Dogs will also react to the tone of our voice when we are getting frustrated and they are trying to keep their head down until we have calmed down. It could also be that they are concentrating hard on what they are doing, chasing or scenting a rabbit or deer for instance; they literally do not hear our call. A dog in a highly aroused state will also be unable to respond to his name, such as a mature male after a bitch in season or a very territorial dog guarding his garden. An absolutely terrified dog will be completely oblivious to everything.

As with all training, if your dog thinks something is worthwhile he will respond enthusiastically.

Sit on cue

Sit is one of the simplest control exercises and one of the easiest to train. It comes naturally for a dog to sit in an alert position when expecting something to happen, such as being given food, the owner's return after leaving, or any exciting interaction such as a ball game. The sit/alert position is preferable to the alternative pulling on the lead, jumping up or milling around in excitement when anticipating an event. As with all training it is important that your dog fully understands what is expected of him, so you need to be patient and ready to repeat the training over a period of time until your dog sits instantly on one command and without a food lure.

Initial training of any exercise should be undertaken with minimum distractions so your dog can concentrate on what you are asking him to do. This is also helpful to you as a trainer, as you then only have to cope with explaining to your dog what you would like him to do. If your dog is looking at next door's cat sitting on the garden fence he will not be interested in learning a new trick, however exciting and rewarding you try to make the exercise.

It is better to have short interesting training sessions several times a day rather than allowing your dog to become bored with one long session. Longer training sessions are acceptable if you have a dog that is very keen or if you are a natural motivator and can keep your dog interested and excited by the training.

If you teach a person to carry out a task they will usually be able to repeat the job in a different location providing they have the right tools. This ability is known as generalizing behaviour. Dogs do not generalize as readily as people and different breeds and individual dogs generalize at different rates. This means that if you teach your dog to sit in the living room, you will have to go through the same training in five or six (more in some cases) different places before he generalizes and understands that 'sit' means the same thing in the garden, the park, your friend's house, the vet's surgery, etc. This is why you will often find at dog training classes that some owners say 'he does it at home', when he will not follow commands in a class situation with many distractions around. He is not being naughty; he just has not been trained properly in enough different locations. It will usually take a shorter time for your dog to understand what you are teaching him each time.

If your dog is fed on a dried complete food, this is ideal for training; using part of his dinner will prevent him from becoming overweight! If your dog is not interested in training for some of his usual food then increase the value of the titbits used. Some dogs are just not that food motivated and you need to find something he likes. When using some of your dog's dinner for training only part of his normal diet should be used, not extra portions. Training with food rewards is the simplest way to show your dog what you want him to do, so if your dog is fed a food that is not easy to use as training rewards then use healthy options such as sausage, cheese, or cook some training treats yourself. If using titbits it is important to adjust your dog's normal feeding to take into account the extra food he is being given during training.

Praise should always be used in conjunction with other rewards and the praise should be given before the food or game. Ideally a short praise word such as 'good' should be used as it helps your dog to understand exactly what he has done correctly. If you use a jumble of words it is not very clear to your dog and you will end up confusing him. Once you have highlighted the behaviour you are pleased with by using your short praise word, you can talk to him as much as you like and use as many words as you like, as he will find this exciting and pleasant even if he does not understand what you are saying.

Teaching a sit

Put your dog on the lead. This is simply to keep your dog near you and to help him concentrate. It should not be used to yank him around.

You should already have taught your dog that when you say his name he needs to pay attention to you.

First of all say your dog's name and reward him for giving you attention. Once you have gained his attention take a titbit and hold it on the end of his nose and lift the hand holding the food (still at the end of his nose) in a forward and upward direction until the dog's back legs start to bend as though he is going to sit. Do not allow him to have the reward until his back end has at least started to tip downwards.

If he starts to jump up for the food just ignore this behaviour completely and remove the titbit until he settles again. Repeat the exercise until he understands that the only way to get the titbit is by dipping his back end – increasing the movement towards the sit position over several repetitions. In many cases the dog will automatically sit quite quickly. As soon as his bottom hits the ground you can go overboard with praise and reward. It is important that you praise him immediately and do not worry as this stage if he stands up straight away afterwards.

Keep repeating this exercise until simply holding the reward in your hand causes him to sit in anticipation. As soon as you are able to keep your dog's attention during training, the lead can be removed.

Now put the titbit in your left hand behind your back and using your right hand guide the dog into the sit position as if you still had a titbit in your hand (as described above). As soon as he sits, praise him and produce the titbit from the left hand. Repeat this several times varying the hiding place of the reward until your dog will sit as soon as you stand in front of him and give the signal. You can even put the titbits on a table near by and teach your dog that he has to sit on cue without any reward being on your person. Change the reward so that sometimes he gets a titbit, sometimes a game and sometimes only praise. On the occasions when praise is his only reward you must make it exciting so that he is not disappointed that he is not getting his food or game.

Only now should you label or put his action on cue. That means that when you give the signal based on the food lure described above, he sits immediately. Now when he sits you can say 'sit', using a firm but kind tone of voice, which differs from the exciting voice you use for praise. Do not say 'sit' until he is in the sitting position. You are labelling that position. If you say 'sit' when the dog is standing it is confusing for him.

Repeat this a number of times and then you can test him to see if he really understands the meaning of the sit. Say 'sit' once with the hand signal that will have developed during the training with the food lure. Do not repeat the word, but if he does not sit immediately, wait whilst holding eye contact with him until he sits. Then go overboard with praise and reward. It is important not to repeat the cue unless you think he has not heard you for some reason. If you get into the habit of repeating a cue for a behaviour the dog will assume that he only has to react after two or three repetitions.

If you wait for some time and he does not respond to the cue 'sit' then you have not done sufficient basic training and you should go back one or two steps. If he sits immediately on cue then reward him heavily. Repeat the test without using the hand signal and again reward him heavily if he responds correctly and quickly.

If you find that your dog will only sit with both the verbal and hand signal, then gradually fade out the hand signal reducing the original exaggerated movement over a period until you do not need to use it at all.

You can now start to extend the time he sits. The aim is for him to maintain the position until you release him verbally with your chosen release word or phrase, for example 'go' or 'OK'. Obviously you must be reasonable in the length of time you ask him to remain sitting.

To extend the time he sits, simply introduce the release word. To start with you will be praising him immediately he sits, then delay the praise very slightly and use your chosen release word just before the praise. Remember that your praise word will be the single word that marks the required behaviour. If he gets up before you give the release word, do not tell him off. Simply ignore his action and ask him to sit again. Very gradually build up the length of time between giving the cue, him sitting, and you giving the release word until he has a rock solid instant sit on cue until released.

When you have an instant extended sit in your normal training area, don't forget you need to repeat the training in as many different places as possible and gradually introduce distractions. When you are training the 'sit' in a new environment it is often helpful to increase the reward to counteract the increased difficulty your dog will have. For example, a piece of cheese, tasty hotdog or chicken might well be delicious enough to get your dog's attention even when other exciting things are going on around him, whereas a boring dry biscuit will hold less attraction.

Ideally you should be in control of the distractions to start with. This means that you set them up with friends and family. For example, your dog should still sit if another family member comes into the room. You can then ask him to sit when members of the family come into the room and move around or talk to each other. You can build on this using willing family and friends and other well-behaved dogs. Be creative, think of different distractions and locations where you would like your dog to sit instantly on cue, and train with this in mind.

Down

This is one of the most useful control exercises to teach your dog, second only to the recall. Teaching your dog to lie down instantly on command is not only impressive for onlookers but can make life a lot easier and safer for both dog and owner.

If you meet a small child or a nervous adult when you are out walking your dog, the down position is much less threatening than a dog running around barking. If you have to attend to an emergency, for instance, if someone has fallen over and you need to help, how much safer for everyone if you can tell your dog to lie down whilst you attend to the problem. Supposing you see some unforeseen danger whilst your dog is off the lead – how reassuring to know that you can stop him in his tracks with a distant down command.

For some breeds, such as Border collies, the down is a default position. For others, like lurchers who have very deep chests, the down is not necessarily the comfortable position and may be harder to train. There are two down positions – the alert ready to move 'down', where the dog holds his body straight, rests on his elbows and holds his head up, and there is the relaxed 'down' where he relaxes on to one side or the other, which naturally bends his body slightly and lowers the head. The alert down is usually the first position, but most dogs will go into the relaxed down if they remain down for any length of time. The relaxed down is preferable for a stay.

From an early age you can start teaching your dog what the word 'down' means. To do this, simply say the word 'down' whenever you see him in the down position. Make sure that a pleasant experience always follows, either a gentle stroke or some calm praise. 'Down – what a good dog!' You could even drop a treat between his front feet.

Try and make training as much fun as possible and remember that your dog does not speak English, so you have to communicate with him in a way that he will understand. Body language is the most readily understood form of communication between a dog and his owner and food is the simplest way to reward your dog's attempts to carry out your instruction.

Some dogs, like labradors, are highly motivated by any food, from a dry crust to a piece of steak. Others may be more discerning and you might need to change the value of the food according to the effort he makes. The ideal food reward is the dog's dinner. You can use part of his dinner for training and when he does something really clever or even if you think he is trying really hard, you give a jackpot reward by letting him eat the rest of his dinner.

If yours is one of the unusual dogs who is not interested in food and you have tried all sorts of different treats, cheese, sausage, etc, then you will have to look more deeply into what he might find rewarding. Perhaps he likes to play tuggy, chase a ball, or just have his chest rubbed.

Whatever reward you are going to offer, you need a word that is short and sweet that you can use to mark the fact that he has done something that you like. 'Good' is the most commonly used. This differs from the usual 'Good dog, what a good dog', because it is much more precise and tells the dog exactly at what point he got it right. You can still praise your dog as part of his reward (and indeed you should) after you have used the 'good' reward marker.

Teaching the down

Choose a training area where there are no distractions. If your dog has already learned to pay attention to you when you are in training mode, then training can take place off the lead. If he is still very easily distracted then it might help to keep him on the lead to start with.

First of all, say your dog's name in a light-hearted voice and praise him when he gives you attention. Take your chosen food reward and show it to the dog. Enclose the food with your hand so that your fingers are downwards. Hold the hand with the food in it under the dog's nose keeping it about half an inch away. Move your hand towards the floor, keeping the food close to his nose and enclosed by your fingers.

When your hand is on the floor and your dog's nose is at the same level give him the food. Do not use the cue 'down' yet. He will learn the behaviour and then you can label it. This makes it easier for the dog to understand exactly what the down position is.

Repeat the exercise but this time do not let him have the food until either he is lying down or has at least crouched down more than the first time. He will be snuffling around your hand trying to get at the food, and you will come in contact with a fair bit of slobber in the process. Surgical gloves are the answer for the squeamish or faint hearted.

Repeat this procedure making him crouch down more each time before releasing the food reward. Smaller dogs will often go into the down position straight away but bigger dogs may do it in progressive stages – don't worry if it takes several attempts. You need to be patient and make sure that you only release the food in response to a definite attempt towards lying down.

The first time the dog goes into the down position it is *very* important that you say 'good' immediately, then give him the food and be wildly enthusiastic with your praise. Don't worry if he gets up straight away – you will be able to extend the length of time he stays down in due course.

In the next training session, repeat the above. He should go into the down position much more quickly this time. Still using the food, bend down less and less each time until you can stand up and just point to the floor and he goes down. Continue to use the 'good' to mark what he has done right and follow this with the food and praise. If you do not fade the hand signal quickly, you will find that you always have to bend down to indicate to the dog that you want him to lie down, which detracts from the usefulness of the exercise.

Now you can introduce the cue word. When you point to the floor and the dog drops, say 'down' immediately followed by 'good' and then the food reward. Repeat this over and over until he drops very quickly. Now leave the food reward on a nearby table or hide it behind your back and repeat the signal. Give him the reward. You now have the start of a 'down' hand signal.

Next, you are ready to test whether he really understands what you have been teaching him. Say 'down' and wait. Do not repeat the cue, just watch your dog and you will see his brain working. Do not allow him to wander off. After a while (it may take minutes) he will go down. Immediately say 'good' and reward. Even if you think he has laid down because he was fed up with waiting for you to speak to him again, this will have helped him to understand the cue.

Repeat the cue and reward several times but stop before he gets bored.

If after waiting for quite a while he does not seem to have the slightest idea what to do, backtrack slightly and repeat earlier lessons. Re-test in the next training session.

Once your dog drops into the down position on cue you can start extending the time that he stays there. To do this simply delay the 'good' slightly. Gradually extend the time until he learns that once told to lie down he must stay there until released. With this method of training most dogs will look on 'good' as the release word. If you wish you could introduce a different release word such as 'OK' or 'go'. To do this use the release word before the 'good' in the same way that you used the 'down' cue before the 'good'.

When you are happy with your dog's understanding of the 'down' cue, you should no longer need the short 'good', but your dog will always need a reward of some sort whether it be verbal or physical praise, food or games. It is just like saying thank you when someone has done something for you that you like.

If you are unable to use food as a reward it may be more difficult to train the down position if the dog does not naturally use the down position. First of all he needs to be conditioned to the reward values of the toy or petting that you are going to use. The toy should be a special toy that is only used for training. When the training session is over, the toy should be removed and put out of reach until the next session. Your dog needs to really want the toy or ball and the game needs to be exciting and fun.

The petting needs to be accompanied by praise so that it is a really good experience for the dog. Watch his reactions and make sure that he really does like what you are doing. Rubbing his chest might be more acceptable than stroking his head, or he may prefer to have his back scratched. Stroking his head might not be a good experience as this can be intimidating for some dogs.

If using a toy, get him really excited by play and then hold the toy in the air in a tantalizing manner. In his frustration he will probably offer a number of behaviours such as jumping up, sitting, pawing and barking in order to get you to continue the game. Ignore all of these. As soon as he offers the down position, let him have the toy and play a wild game with him. Once he understands that the down position is what gets the reward you can proceed as with food training. This method can also be used to introduce a hand signal for a distant down. For instance, holding the toy in the air can be changed to holding your hand in the air. This signal is visible from quite a long distance. It can also be used to train the instant down and down on the move when the dog has mastered the basic down.

Whilst holding the toy in the air, call the dog, when he is running towards you, cue the down, and throw him the toy as soon as he drops into position. Play an exciting game. As the training progresses you can delay throwing the toy so that he learns that he has to maintain the position until released.

Remember that you need to be in control of the games and you need to be able to stop whenever you want to – not when the dog decides. It is an important part of teaching self-control.

When your dog fully understands the cue where there are no distractions, you need to retrain the exercise in at least six different places, gradually introducing more and more distractions. Maybe you started the training in your living room when the family had all gone out for the evening. Next it could be in the garden, then the park or perhaps a friend's garden. Distractions can be people, noises, other dogs, aeroplanes overhead, motorbikes roaring past and all sorts of other everyday happenings.

Do not be discouraged if your dog does not immediately understand the cue in a new place. You may well have to completely or partly retrain him in each venue, but it will be quicker each time. You will know that he fully understands the cue the first time you take him somewhere new to train and he drops into the down position immediately when asked. If he does – take him out to the pub for a drink and a slap-up meal, because this is really brilliant!

Most of all, make all training fun for you and your dog.

Stand

The stand is an exercise that is often overlooked or only seen as useful to teach if you are thinking of showing your dog, or taking part in obedience type training and are thinking of entering competitions. But the stand is an extremely useful exercise in many ways, for example if your dog can stand in position while the vet carries out a heath check, including taking his temperature, feeling his abdomen – something that is impossible if your dog sits as a displacement behaviour when he is worried about something. If you can ask your dog to stand and he knows exactly what stand means it is one less thing for him to worry about. This is preferable to trying to fight him into position and cause him untold stress by trying to hold him up in the stand position while the vet does what he has to do.

Stand is useful when you need to dry your dog, groom him, take burs and grass seeds out of his coat, inspect him for lumps or bumps.

Teaching the stand is very easy. Hold a small titbit between your finger and thumb and with your dog in the sit, bring the titbit slowly forward in a straight line. When your dog stands use your praise word 'good' and give your dog his titbit. You only want your dog to stand not walk, so move slowly. The way that you move your hand with the titbit then becomes your hand signal for the stand. When your dog is moving into the stand without hesitation, this is the time to put the behaviour on cue. Move your hand forward, as your dog *begins* to stand, say 'stand', and reward. Again, begin in a place without distractions before moving on to other places and situations to practise.

Walking on a loose lead

Lead walking is often a controversial exercise as there are so many ways of stopping a dog from pulling, including some very useful training aids, some of which we will explore. Firstly we need to establish what the owner wants. Is it a dog that sticks to the leg like Velcro as though doing obedience at Crufts? Or a walk that the owner and dog can enjoy together without the owner having their arm wrenched out of its socket and the dog choking on the collar? Most owners want the latter and that is what this section aims to achieve.

Before we work on the actual exercise we need to have a little understanding about why dogs pull. Is it because they are excited about where they are going? Is it because they want to be in front all the time? Are they being dominant? I believe that the answer is that the owner has *taught* their dog to pull! Albeit inadvertently. Look at what happens the first time a lead and collar are put on a puppy, the owner invariably winds the lead around their hand and makes the lead taut, then when the puppy pulls towards something they follow, the puppy stops and has a sniff and then pulls towards something else, the owner either follows *or* pulls the puppy in another direction. The puppy has learned that strength matters, if you want to get to something or go somewhere you need to pull and if that doesn't work then you need to pull harder! Consider how dogs and puppies learn, they learn through experience and reward, if the experience is rewarding then they are more likely to repeat it. If pulling on the lead results in your dog/puppy getting to what it wants, that is reward enough. Randomly reward any behaviour and it strengthens! So sometimes allowing your dog to pull and other times not allowing him to pull will only strengthen the pulling behaviour! By the time your dog is an adult he is a seasoned puller, which often results in your dog not been taken for a walk, as it is too uncomfortable for the owner.

Traditional methods, such as those used by the late Barbara Woodhouse, relied on aversive methods to train 'heel work'. A choke chain was worn by your dog which meant that it could only be walked on one side, usually the left, and when your dog walked out in front, the owner was instructed to shout 'heel' and then jerk your dog back to their side. This type of training relies on your dog learning to avoid the aversive of the choke chain tightening, your dog hears the 'heel' command and waits for the jerk and then returns to the owner's side. Eventually some dogs learn to remain by the owner's side in order to avoid the uncomfortable jerk, others spend a lifetime being pulled and jerked around.

Development in dog training has led to a better understanding of how dogs learn and how best to train them. There are various methods used by trainers teaching lead walking and numerous pieces of equipment that promise to stop dogs pulling, some of which will be discussed.

Let's look at some of the techniques used by modern trainers.

1 As your dog gets to the end of the lead, you should stop walking, call your dog back to your side, praise your dog and continue walking, repeating the whole process again.

2 Very similar to number 1. As your dog gets to the end of the lead you should stop and walk backwards until your dog rejoins you, praise and continue the walk, repeating the process.

3 When your dog gets to the end of the lead, stop, call your dog back, turn and walk back a pace, turn and continue in the original direction praising when your dog is next to you, repeat.

4 Immediately your dog starts to pull, turn around and go back home.

The drawback of 1, 2 and 3 is that they may set up a pattern of behaviour like a yo-yo effect. Collies love repetitive behaviour and will go to the end of the lead and come back to the side ad infinitum, they think that this is what you are teaching them! Other dogs will do the same, some may inhibit the pulling but still go to the end of the lead in anticipation of being called back to start again! Number 4 would be good for a lot of dogs and puppies, they would learn that the consequences of pulling meant the abrupt end to the walk, but only if they are on the outward journey and near enough to home for the connection to be made. It may also set up a lot of frustration especially for a young puppy that is just excited about going out into the big wide world. It would be useless for a dog that pulls on the way home! These methods are designed to show your dog what we don't want, i.e. when your dog pulls the walk is momentarily stopped or terminated.

There are training aids that are designed to stop pulling, certain head collars and harnesses can be used and for some dogs and owners this is the answer, but most owners find that a determined puller can learn to pull even on one of these. They are great to use to give you a window in which to work. In between your training sessions when you have to get from A to B and cannot spare the time to work with your dog, a head collar or stop pull harness will help by reducing the stress on the owner. However, there is no substitute for 'good training'.

What is the answer? The method below is suitable for both puppies new to lead walking and dogs that have learnt to pull well. It may sound a little convoluted at times, however, it works very well.

In order for your dog or puppy to change, you have to make changes. You must learn to use your voice and body language and not the lead (except in emergencies). Firstly, you must learn to stand still with your dog on the lead and not pull your dog back to you or allow your dog to move you off the spot, get your dog's attention by using your voice, try making a kissing noise (this generally gets a dog's attention), when he looks back at you encourage your dog to you and praise, spend several minutes practising this, you should see a change in the way your dog stands on the lead, he should no longer lean into the lead but stand relaxed. Now try a little experiment. Put a little pressure on the lead by pulling gently, watch how your dog leans into the lead in order to remain where he is, it's now up to you to practise the new method.

The equipment you will need for the lead walking are, an ordinary flat collar (no choke chains), a training lead approximately six feet in length, or a belt and an ordinary length lead, a clicker and lots of treats. You will find in Chapter 08 how to introduce and use the clicker, you could use a clicker word, such as 'bingo', 'yes' or 'good' but this may reduce the effectiveness of the training as you probably speak to your dog a lot in an effort to stop him pulling, so he may not make the connection quickly enough.

Firstly, you are going to use just the collar and lead. Try and work in an area that gives you space but not too many distractions. Walk forward and as soon as your dog gets to the end of the lead stop (sound familiar!), do not pull your dog but get his attention, as soon as he looks around turn and encourage your dog with you and continue in the opposite direction, repeat. This will just give you the rhythm and let your dog know that pulling no longer works, when you have tried this for several minutes have a break. Now you are going to let your dog know what is the required behaviour through rewards.

Because you will need two hands, one for the clicker and one for the treats, the next stage will require you to attach your dog's lead to your waist! The exceptions to this are, if you have a back problem or if you have one of the giant breeds such as a Great Dane that may pull you over, in which case use a stop pull harness instead of the collar and use a belt and lead instead of the training lead, as this tightens a little at first until your dog gets used to not pulling. Alternatively, you could employ someone of a larger frame to assist with the training.

If you have the normal length lead and the belt, put the belt on and attach the lead to the belt. If you are using a training lead, put the lead around your waist, thread it though the handle and attach it to your dog. You now have two hands free to use the clicker and treats. You will also find that now you do not have your hands on the lead your dog does not pull as much! Begin the walking again, this time as you turn and walk in the opposite direction and your dog is walking near you and not pulling, click and treat. If your dog is going to walk on the left side of you have treats in the left hand and the clicker in the right, this will make it easier to administer the treat. As you move forward try not to stop to give the treat when you have clicked but keep moving and reward as you go. When your dog moves away from you to the end of the lead, stop again, begin to turn and use your voice to coax your dog to change direction with you, once he is walking by you again click and treat. After a few trials you should see that your dog is choosing to be near you in order to get the click and treat and that you are getting further and further along the path. At first you will be clicking every two or three paces, then you can gradually increase the number of paces you take to six or seven with your dog on a slack lead before you next click and treat. Within your first session your dog should begin to understand what you want, you should see your dog begin to inhibit the pulling and walk more and more by your side or near you. You are now giving your dog the information about what you *do* want. The experience is rewarding for both of you! Pitfalls to avoid at this stage include: rewarding you dog as he rejoins you from the end of the lead, he must get at least one pace next to you before you click and treat. You may find a tendency to 'lure' your dog by holding the food for him to follow, avoid this, and keep the hand with the food in up by your waist making sure that you only move it towards your dog after you have clicked your clicker.

You will need to practise this for two or three days several times a day, never allowing your dog to pull. Hopefully you will see that your dog is walking better for longer and that the clicker is used only after completing some 10–20 and then 20–30 paces. Practice sessions should be kept reasonably short, it is better to have three or four ten-minute training sessions where your dog does not pull, than 30 minutes, of which most of the journey your dog is allowed to pull sometimes. Avoid outings where your dog will be distracted too much to concentrate on training, such as journeys to the school and back with young children around. This outing can be done when you have better lead work.

On day four or five, depending on the amount of practice you have been doing, you can try leaving the lead in your hands and keeping the clicker in your pocket. This is where the training lead is an advantage; it will enable you to allow your dog just that little extra length to sniff the pavement or grass without the lead going tight. Should your dog get to the end of the lead and pull just go back to turning around and going in the opposite direction for a short while, but do not go back to your old ways of pulling your dog. Put the lead around your waist and get the clicker out again if you feel that your dog needs some further reinforcement.

You may feel that turning and going in the opposite direction every few yards is going to look silly, or you may think that all you want to do is take your dog for a walk and you are never going to get to the end of the road! The turning and going in the opposite direction will only last a short time and it is worth the time and effort especially if you have a dog that has been pulling for some time. If you are concerned that your puppy is not getting exercise, consider that very young puppies do not need 'exercise'. They need time out in the environment, learning how to walk nicely so that when they are older they can be taken for longer walks! Remember that you can use the training aids that were discussed earlier for the times when you have not got time for training.

Never try to train more than one dog at a time or train an untrained dog next to a trained dog.

If you find that you get outside and your dog does not want to take food from you, you may need to do some remedial training before lead work can commence. You may need to improve your relationship with your dog; this can be done through play.

This is a little exercise that may help both you and your dog to understand that pulling no longer works. Have your dog on a training lead, have some treats in your free hand, throw a treat on the floor within your dog's reach without the lead going tight. When your dog has picked up the treat he should look back to you, as he does throw him another treat within his lead radius, watch for him picking it up and looking at you for another treat. Repeat this several times always waiting for your dog to look at you before you throw another treat. The next treat needs to be thrown outside of your dog's reach so hold the lead just a fraction shorter without making it tight, throw the treat and be prepared for your dog to try to pull towards it, stand your ground and wait … your dog will watch the treat for a few seconds, hopefully he will then look back at you, great!

Immediately you should go forward with your dog keeping the lead really slack and allow your dog to pick up the treat. Repeat the whole exercise again. What your dog should be learning is that when something he wants is out of reach, he must look back at his owner to get permission to go and get it! This exercise can be very useful if you practise it using other things such as toys as the item thrown out of your dog's reach. It should also begin to teach your dog some patience. Another use of this exercise is to progress it so that when your dog looks back for permission to go to something and you don't want your dog to, you can put in a 'leave it' command and reward your dog for moving back to you and walking away from the item of interest.

Stay

Stay means 'stay exactly where you are without moving until I come back to you'. This is different from the 'wait', which means 'wait where you are until I tell you to do something else' and 'settle', which is telling your dog to find somewhere comfortable to settle down.

If you wish to take part in The Kennel Club Good Citizen Dog Scheme Club Tests, Obedience, Agility, Working Trials, Gundog Tests and many other doggy activities your dog will need to understand the 'stay' command. On a practical day-to-day level it is extremely useful if you can depend on your dog to stay in one place. Stay is useful in an emergency, for example, if you need to deal with an accident or if you smashed a bottle of milk on the kitchen floor. It can also be used when you meet a friend on a walk and stop for a chat and it really helps to have a good stand/stay for grooming. A dog that you can trust to stay in one place whilst you are busy dealing with something else is a pleasure to live with.

Teaching the 'stay' will teach your dog to have confidence in you and to have confidence in himself and to listen to what you say. You may have spent a lot of time teaching your dog to come to you from a distance and follow you when you move, he is now confident to stay on his own.

There are two elements to a stay – time and distance – both of which have to be carefully and slowly taught. You are aiming to reward your dog for maintaining the 'stay' position, not correct him for moving, so take it slowly.

The following describes how to teach the sit/stay. The same method applies for the 'down' and 'stand' stays. Concentrate on only one 'stay' position during a training session. Trying to teach a down stay directly after a sit stay will only confuse your dog, leading him to change position in an effort to try and understand what you want. Only once your dog is very thoroughly trained would you expect him to be able to stay in different positions following each other. Dogs who compete in obedience competitions hold the stay in different positions following on from each other, but even they quite often get it wrong.

Once your dog has learnt to sit on command without a food lure, you can start to teach the 'sit/stay'. As with all exercises, always train something new without distractions. When you gradually introduce distractions (other dogs, people, etc.) go back to a stage you know your dog can do easily. Always tell your dog to 'sit/stay' rather than just 'stay', or he may become confused when you introduce other positions.

Training can be done either on or off lead.

Teach your dog to sit beside you, slowly building up the time, second by second, praising your dog for sitting ('Good sit/stay', 'That's a good sit/stay', 'What a good dog') and feeding him titbits every so often. Always aim to release your dog before he moves. By repeating the command 'sit/stay' when your dog is staying he will form an association between what you are saying and what he is doing.

Once your dog can sit beside you for about 30 seconds, start to move away from your dog either to the front or to the side whilst he is sitting. Continue to verbally praise him while he is still sitting and staying. To start with only leave your dog for one or two seconds before returning to him. When you return to your dog give him a food treat as a reward and then give him the release command to signal that it's the end of the exercise. Initially your dog may well move when you leave him, so be ready to put him back into the sit and re-command him to 'sit/stay', praising him as soon as he sits. If he breaks the sit/stay when you try and move away from him he may not understand what stay means. The secret is to move away and back within a second at first, so that your dog does not even have time to move.

Continue to increase both the time and the distance from your dog in very small stages. Every time you increase the distance return immediately to your dog and reward and release. Then ask him to 'sit/stay' for a gradually longer time at that distance, returning to him every so often to praise and reward him with a treat, re-command him and leave him again without releasing him. It is important to be able to reward your dog for doing the exercise. If you try to increase time and distance together you will make it too difficult for your dog.

Teaching the 'stay' can be very frustrating if your dog keeps moving. It is important therefore that you only progress at your dog's pace. In the early stages it is tempting to 'test' your dog by leaving him for too long or at too great a distance. If you do this it is more than likely he will get up and walk away! The more chance your dog has of getting it wrong, the longer it will take for him to get it right, so try to ensure that he succeeds on every occasion you leave him.

Wait

Many dog owners, who have almost no control over their dog's behaviour in all other circumstances, will proudly tell me that they can get their dog to sit and wait whilst his dinner is put down and not touch it until told to do so. This seems to be teaching a behaviour in the most difficult of situations. A hungry dog who is under no form of control, being trained to sit and wait when he is at his most excitable, dinner being a major event to most dogs, yet when you ask how the owner how they taught this they cannot explain the step-by-step process. Nor have they been able to transfer this amount of control to any other aspect of the dog's life.

Teaching a dog to wait until further instructions, or permission to carry on with what he is doing, can be very useful in many areas of your day-to-day existence with your pet.

The introduction of a wait command can be done by holding the dog's collar, or holding him on a short lead, and placing a piece of food on the floor just out of reach. Do not begin with best liver, which he will spend a considerable amount of time and effort trying to reach but preferably with a piece of lowest value food that your dog will work for. With a dog that is not much interested in food you may have to resort to the liver, but a breed such as a labrador will probably sell his soul for a piece of dog biscuit. Hold on to the dog's collar and say nothing until you feel him relax, then count to three, say 'wait' in a calm conversational tone, and then pick up the reward and give it to him. If you are using a clicker, then click and reward. Don't introduce the word 'wait' until you are getting your dog to stand calmly for the required three seconds almost every time. By giving the reward yourself and not letting your dog just get it himself you are actively reinforing the act of waiting. Gradually increase the time before the dog gets the reward until you take your hand off his collar and leave him sitting (or standing, the position is not important) for a full minute before getting the reward. Repeat this training in as many different places as you can, i.e. the kitchen, lounge, garden, etc.

You can introduce this cue into situations where it will be useful in your everyday dealings with your dog. The most useful one being, wait and allow me to go through the door first. How annoying it is to be barged aside by a large dog who is keen to get out for his walk, or who wants to get on to the sofa first!

Begin, as with all new exercises, in a situation where you are most likely to succeed. This would not be at walk time whilst standing by the front door with a lead in your hand, but more likely after a long walk, going from the kitchen to the dining room. Assuming that your dog has been taught the wait cue thoroughly, you should approach the door with your dog on a loose lead and ask him to wait, maintain the position for 30 seconds, reward and walk away. He should not be able to predict that a door will be opened every time he walks up to it. Repeat a couple of times, then when he is waiting nicely, reach out and slowly open the door. If he makes any move towards the door close it again and walk away, it will only take a few repetitions before he realizes that getting up will actually remove the expected reward. Once you are able to fully open the door without him moving, walk through the door yourself and invite him to follow. Repeat the wait command whilst you close the door behind you. Practise this on as many internal doors as possible before progressing to the door which leads to the outside and the greatest reward of all – a walk!

Being able to wait getting into and out of the car is of vital importance especially when getting out of the car, as you need to get your dog out under control when he is excited about his walk and where there may be other cars, dogs and people. The easiest option is getting into the car; remember to start with the easiest option first. With the lead on walk up to the car and give the wait command. Open the door and reward him for not jumping in, walk away and repeat. After a couple of repetitions, provided you have been successful in obtaining a good calm wait, you can now ask him to jump in. Again, give the wait command and ask him to jump out. Do not shut the door between the jump in and jump out requests as this will mean a period of time when you are not in control. Once he has successfully completed this exercise three or four times take him indoors and give him his dinner, or a game. Do not immediately take him in the car for a walk, as this will increase his excitement levels next time he approaches the car. Once he is happily waiting to get in and out with the door open then you can progress to closing the door.

Having got a good wait before jumping in, give him permission to get in and shut the door initially with the lead still attached, and count to ten. Repeat the wait command and open the door. Any move to jump out without being asked to will result in you shutting the door and walking away. Return after two minutes and repeat.

Once he is waiting for the door to be opened remove his lead when he gets in and be sure that he waits to have his lead attached before giving permission to get out. After repeating this several times again take him inside and feed or play. Repeat this exercise in your drive, in quiet car parks, or at friends' houses. Of course, whilst teaching this exercise it will probably be necessary to take him in the car for his walk. If you are not able to reinforce the training, *do not* use the wait command, but keep his lead on whilst in the car and physically restrain him from jumping out. As with all training, if you own more than one dog this will need to be taught individually to a high standard before trying to get both dogs to wait in the car at the same time.

Waiting whilst off lead in the park is useful should your dog get too far ahead, or you just want him to stand still because there are other dogs or people approaching. The easiest option is to teach this whilst the dog is running towards you, however the teaching of this exercise will require an assistant. Husbands, wives, partners and children make good assistants. Having already taught the concept of wait the dog should be happy to wait in the sit or down position whilst you walk away. If you can't do this don't worry, it will just mean another assistant to hold onto his collar. You will need some food rewards in a container, or a favourite toy. Walk away to a distance of about ten yards, and show the dog that you have nothing in your hands, hiding the reward behind you. Position your assistant halfway between you and your dog, at right angles to the dog.

Having called your dog, and providing you have a good recall, when your dog is opposite your assistant throw the reward to him, making a big overarm gesture, like bowling a cricket ball, whilst saying 'wait'. This is to give your dog a visual command as well as a verbal one. If he stops your assistant will give him a piece of food or a game with the toy. If he keeps on coming ignore him and your assistant will entice him back for his reward. Keep repeating this exercise until he puts on the brakes when he sees you raise your arm to throw. At this stage if you are using food give the food to your assistant before commencing the exercise. When you give the wait command use the overarm signal with the flat of the hand being the visual cue, when he stops your assistant will, without making a huge gesture, drop a piece of food just behind his tail.

If you are using a toy you can dispense with your assistant at this stage and use the overarm gesture, together with the command 'wait'. When he stops throw the toy to land just behind his tail. He will think this is a great game and almost be looking for opportunities to wait. Now you can use the command and the toy when he is going in the opposite direction, but again don't make this difficult and try to get a wait when he is off to join in a game of football with local kids in the park! Pick a quiet spot when he is just trotting off to explore by himself. This exercise is much easier if your dog likes to play with toys as they are more easily seen in the fields than pieces of food that can get lost in the grass, and they go further so that you can ask for the wait at a greater distance. Once your dog is doing this reliably do not always reward in the same manner, sometimes the reward is that he can 'go on' and get on with what he was doing. Sometimes you will need to go to him and reward; it may be that you have asked him to wait in order to call him to you to have his lead on. It is useful to practise doing this on walks in order that he cannot predict when his walk will end.

A reliable wait command also gives you greater control over your dog's chase instincts. If you are able to ask your dog to wait whilst you throw a ball and only go when given permission then you can use the same command around other dogs, cats, children, rabbits, etc. Although of course you will not follow it up with permission to 'go get it'. To teach this aspect of the wait command you should already have the behaviour taught reliably in other less exciting situations. Be sure that the toy that you use is a toy which is safe. By that I mean not a tennis ball for a Rottweiler or a small bouncy ball for a staffie. Never throw anything for your dog that may be accidentally swallowed, and never throw sticks, which can splinter in your dog's mouth, or be jabbed into the back of his throat.

With your dog sitting by your side loop his lead through his collar and hold it without putting pressure on his collar. Give the 'wait' command and throw his toy. Only when your dog is sitting calmly can you let go of one end of the lead and give him permission to go after it. By now when clipping the lead to the collar you are not making it obvious to your dog that he is on the lead, but you can restrain him should he try to take off before being given the release command. When progressing to doing this exercise off lead you will need to employ your trusty assistant again. If you take the lead off, throw the toy and just trust to luck, if your dog breaks the wait position you either have to grab him, which will make him wary and he will quickly become an expert at avoiding the grab, or he will gain a huge reward for not obeying the wait command by getting the toy. With the help of a second person you can remove the reward if he fails to wait and thereby teach him that only if he does as asked will he gain any advantage. Station your assistant approximately where you expect the toy to land, ask your dog to wait and throw his toy. Count to three and give him permission to get it. Should your dog break his position then as soon as he moves your assistant will pick up his toy and throw it back to you whereupon you will have a good game with it yourself, keeping it out of his reach. After a few repetitions he will realize that if he runs in then the reward will be removed and he will not be allowed to have it. By playing with it yourself you are increasing his desire for his toy and he will then be prepared to work harder (wait longer) to get it in the end.

Recall

The recall is the most important exercise that you can teach your dog or puppy. If you can't let your dog off the lead because you worry that he might not come back, he is then destined to a life on the lead whenever he goes out. This will reduce his social skills with other dogs as he needs freedom to meet and greet. Being kept on the lead will also increase frustration and reduce opportunities to explore his environment, which is necessary for mental stimulation.

So then, why do so many people find this exercise so difficult? Let's look firstly at what a recall should mean. As an owner you should be able to call your dog and your dog should respond by returning to you! Why do so many dogs not comply? There are two main reasons; firstly, he has never been taught to recall, owners just expect that if they call their dog's name, their dog will return to them. Maybe he will if there are no other distractions! Secondly, your dog will often associate the call with the end of fun and freedom and decide that he would rather stay in the park playing with other dogs or investigating his environment. This 'disobedience' can lead to frustration on the part of you, the owner, who may use 'punishment' of sorts such as shouting at or even hitting your dog. This just reinforces your dog's absent behaviour, what dog wants to return to an owner who is unpleasant? Understanding this will help you with the recall programme.

So, firstly, we need to *teach* a recall and not just expect your dog to 'know' what to do, and secondly, we need to make the recall a very rewarding experience.

It is important to remember that the 'reward' needs to be what your *dog* sees as rewarding, not what *you* think it might be. There is little contest between dried kibble and tasty meat offcuts or baked liver! The harder the work, i.e. doing a recall away from other dogs, the bigger and better the reward needs to be during training. You may consider that your affection, patting and soft vocal tones are rewarding, but your dog may get these throughout the day for the merest compliance or for just 'being', so it doesn't have the same 'value' as maybe a tasty treat that is produced at odd times. You may find that for some dogs food takes second place to a game with a ball or tuggie. If your dog has a favourite toy and you keep it special by only allowing limited access to it, this will also act as a high grade reward. If at present your dog is not particularly interested in a toy then start playing several times a day and having fun with your dog, keep the toy special by putting it aside until the next time you play. Knowing what your dog finds rewarding is the first step to a successful recall.

Training puppies

If you are training a puppy then your job is much easier. Puppies have a natural inbuilt insecurity and when very young do not want to be away from their attachment figure, so getting them off lead early will help progress your recall. If you have not had your puppy off lead by the time he is five months then you will need to be vigilant as they begin to gain confidence and will go that much further. Avoid chasing any loose puppy, they will always run away from you. If in doubt than use a long line until your recall is well practised. When you are practising, use trees to hide behind, as long as you can keep an eye on your puppy and put a little doubt in your puppy's mind about where you are, this will teach him to check where you are periodically.

Understanding

If is often thought that dogs are deliberately disobedient, they run off, and when you call them they ignore you. Let's look at a different opinion. Imagine that you are watching the television and it's your favourite programme or an interesting news report, then suddenly a family member says loudly, 'Are you listening to me? I'm talking to you'. The answer is no you weren't listening; you could not fully concentrate on more than one thing at a time!

Now understand that your dog, when he's out in the field taking in all that information through his senses, all those smells, all those sounds, his concentration is fully taken up with processing that information and it is hard for him to hear your calls.

If, while you were watching that television programme the phone rang, that would break through your level of concentration and you would respond. The same as having taught a good recall and introduced a whistle in the correct way, your dog will find it difficult *not* to respond.

The following recall progamme is designed in three stages; each needs to be worked on before moving to the next. The aim is to have a dog who will come on the first calling, not one that comes when you have called three, four, five or six times. Read the whole programme before you start and keep a note on how well each stage is going so that you can see the progress your dog is making.

First stage

This stage is for any dog of any age, irrespective of previous learning, so if you have a puppy that has not started training or an older dog that comes back 'sometimes', you start here!

You will need treats (really tasty and no bigger than a quarter of a choc drop), a favourite toy, one your dog gets really excited about, a whistle, this doesn't have to be a 'dog' whistle, it can be a gun dog whistle or a referee's whistle, this way you know how loud it sounds! A long line, possibly a lunge line used for horse training which is available from horse equipment suppliers (not an extending lead, these are not suitable for this exercise) and patience! You will also need to give thought as to what you are going to 'call' to your dog, i.e. your dog's name and the words 'come' or 'here' or 'come here'. This recall phrase will need to be consistent, you cannot begin the training with, for example 'Bonny come' and later shout 'come here Bonny'!

Work in a familiar room that is quiet. Hold the treats so that your dog or puppy can see them and give one or two just to get him interested and to keep his attention. At this point you do not need to say anything. Next, remain where you are and say the recall cue and then give another treat, repeat this several times being sure to say the recall cue *before* you give the treat, not at the same time. You are building an association between the words and the treats. Next, take one step backwards and call once, do not be tempted to call and call, be patient and wait for the response. Some dogs will move immediately, others will stand and work out what it is that you want, but if you have built the association between the recall cue and the treat your dog will respond. That was your first 'one call' recall! Repeat the whole process at least three times. Next, do exactly the same but this time before you give the treat, take the collar, this adds extra control in the early stages, especially for those dogs who previously have come to within a hand's distance from you and run off again!

It is important to reward your dog as soon as he gets to you. Don't ask for your dog to sit, if you do you will be rewarding the sitting and not the recall, later you can add the sit if you want to. Remember, your dog needs to build the association between the recall and the reward. Begin to put a greater distance between you and your dog. Get other family members to join in and play a 'round robin' game remembering to call just once and wait for a response. Your dog may find it hard at first to move away from the one with the treats until he realizes that everyone has treats if he just goes where he's called. Start to move outside and call from outside to inside and vice versa, stopping before your dog loses enthusiasm. This new 'game' can be played any time during the day, you will be working on making this a 'hard-wired' response.

Introducing the whistle

If you want to introduce a whistle this is the best time. The types of dog best suited to the whistle are those that you need to be seen to have good control over, any of the guarding breeds, German shepherd dogs (GSDs), Rottweilers, any type of bull breeds, all large dogs that are known to be overfriendly such as labradors and most terriers, as they have a tendency to run off looking for rabbits!

The whistle will make your recall more reliable as when your dog's attention is fully on other things, the sound of the whistle will interrupt his concentration and bring him back to you.

Decide how you wish to make the whistle sound, just like your recall cue it must be the same every time, try it out without your dog being around. Try one 'peep', try 'peep peep', and see what you prefer. Just before you make your next recall blow the whistle and then call your dog, your dog should recognize the whistle after about four or five recalls. This is now part of your recall and should be used every time you are out. You do not need to use it in the house but a little practice now and again will be beneficial. From now on when we say recall this implies that you should use your whistle if you have chosen to and call. You will notice that your dog is responding as soon as you blow the whistle and already returning to you before you get the 'call' in, but don't drop the recall cue. You need to use the two together for some time to come.

During the first stage you will need to be certain that each call is successful and productive. It will also mean that if you feel that your dog is unlikely to come when called, i.e. when he is very engrossed in something, then you should not call him but go and get him, take a lead with you if need be.

You will be able to practise the recall away from home if the chosen area is safe and free of major distractions such as other dogs. This is the time to use the long line. This will give less confident owners reassurance that they can get hold of their dog quickly should the need arise. Call your dog between two people, you can let go of the line and allow it to drag on the ground as the distance and reliability increases.

This is the stage where you may find the food that you have is less interesting, you may need to increase the palatability, introducing new foods that your dog has not had before. This should keep his interest going for a while. If you have been playing toy games with your dog this is when it will pay dividends. This is the chance to use the toy as a reward. When you next call your dog and he begins to return to you, get his toy out, hopefully a ball on a rope and throw the ball behind you in an excited manner so that your dog sees it and increases his speed in order to chase the ball. This works very well with dogs that like to chase, such as collies, GSDs, terriers and sight hounds.

Practise the first stage until you have a good and sharp response. Begin to reward the quicker responses, for the mediocre ones use just verbal praise.

Stage two

Having taught a good response without distractions, your dog needs to progress to learning the skill of responding with distractions.

Once again you will start in the house. You will know your dog well enough by now to know what he finds distracting. Make it easy to begin with, such as a family member holding food, but not letting your dog have it. You can have your dog on a lead but you must not use the lead to pull the dog away from the distraction. When your dog shows interest in the food being held, recall your dog once, and wait. Watch for any signs of response, call again if necessary, and wait. It is important to allow your dog time to respond, later your dog will respond quicker. As soon as your dog begins to respond, move backwards away from the distraction so that your dog has to follow you. Now play with your dog or give a really tasty treat. Your dog has just worked really hard! Now your dog gets a second reward, he gets to go back to the distraction if he wishes. Repeat the process a few times and then take the distraction you are using away. Your dog will now have learned that coming away from distractions is rewarding!

Practise in the garden with distractions of increasing difficulty, such as children playing ball games or someone holding his favourite toy. You are now ready to take your dog to the park and practise. Take your long line with you, you can either keep your dog on the line or off and call him back before another dog arrives. When you see another dog in the distance and before your dog spots it, call your dog to you. When the other dog comes close enough allow the dogs to meet and greet, making sure that the line does not hamper them or become tight in any way. Once they have met, recall your dog and wait for a response, you may need to call a second time, as soon as your dog responds, produce your toy to play with unless, of course, the food that you have is more rewarding. Treat you dog and tell him he can now go back to the other dog! Repeat the process, this time keeping your dog on the lead and continuing your walk, allowing your dog off the lead once the other dog is out of sight. Should your dog at any time see another dog and you do not have him on the lead, do not call him. He needs lots more practice, you will just have to let him meet the other dog and hope they don't go running off together! Go up to your dog and put the lead on, now you can do a recall and reward any good responses, allowing your dog back to the other dog if appropriate. Practise this stage for a few weeks; the responses should get better, especially if you are playing with your dog when he comes to you. When you feel that 99 per cent of the time your dog will recall away from another dog whilst on the lead you can go on to the second half of this stage. You can now allow your dog to greet other dogs off the lead. As they greet, keep walking and then recall your dog. The first few times that your dog responds make sure that you have a really high grade reward available or make the game particularly exciting.

Stage three

Now that you feel confident about your dog coming away from distractions it is time to increase the difficulty. You will now try and recall before he gets to the other dog/distraction! Make it easy at first, calling when your dog first sees another dog at a distance and as soon as he begins to make a move, rewarding heavily when he returns to you and then allowing your dog to go and see the other one. Once again the dog gets a 'double reward'. Practise this at decreasing distances as your dog's response improves. At times you will be able to allow your dog to go off again, or you will be able to keep him with you by extending the game until the other dog is out of sight. Gradually you will be able to change the types of rewards and the frequency at which they are given, so that your dog will never know what he is coming back for, a tasty reward, a piece of dried dog food, or a game with his favorite toy or just some verbal praise from you. Good luck!

Retrieve

Some dogs love to retrieve a ball or toy, others might chase a toy but are not interested in bringing it back and some aren't even interested in the chase. Some dogs have been put off retrieving when, perhaps, as a puppy they were told off for retrieving a tea towel or another 'treasure' they had come across.

When a dog enjoys retrieving a ball (playing 'fetch'), it is an excellent game to play at the field or even in your garden. It is a good way of exercising your dog and making *you* more interesting to your dog when he is off lead.

When you are teaching the retrieve it is worth remembering that it is in fact a series of actions that you are asking for:

- Go towards the toy.
- Pick the toy up.
- Hold the toy.
- Return to the owner (still holding the toy).
- Stop in front of the owner.
- Hold the toy until the owner asks for a drop or give.
- Drop the toy into the owner's hand (or on the ground if you prefer).

I think you'll agree, for a dog that is not a natural retriever, it is quite a complex exercise.

The easiest way for your dog to learn this exercise is to teach him in reverse order so the first thing you need teach him is the last part of the exercise – drop the toy into your hand or onto the floor.

Don't try to rush the training. It might take two or three sessions for your dog to progress to the final exercise. Interrupt the training before he can get bored and come back to it at a later time.

Offer your dog the toy (do not push the toy into his mouth), if he takes the toy praise him and offer a reward (so he will drop it back into your hand). If he is really not interested in holding the toy try to make it more interesting, run it along the floor like 'prey' for your dog to grab, hide it behind you or perhaps take a great deal of interest in it yourself. One or all of these should make the toy more appealing to your dog. You can then praise and reward him for sniffing and taking an interest in the toy to start with and gradually ask for a little more interest before rewarding. So, reward for a couple of sniffs, then wait for a more enthusiastic sniffing or mouthing before rewarding and soon he should be trying to take the toy into his mouth (for which he should be rewarded enthusiastically).

When he is happily taking the toy from your hand, you can put the toy on your knee or between your knees (if you are sitting down) or on the floor. All being well, he will pick it up and give it to you. Reward and praise heartily. Drop the toy on the floor (close to you) for a few more times until your dog is again comfortable with what is required of him, then increase the distance now and he will happily race after it and bring it back. However, some dogs are not so sure and if you throw the toy 20 feet up in the garden he may ignore it or chase it and then forget what the next bit is. If your dog is like this then take it slowly and increase the distance you are throwing the toy in small stages. If at any point you find the dog loses interest then take the distance back to the one he could cope with, ask him to bring the toy to you and when he does, praise, reward and finish the training session.

If you have a natural retriever you will be able to miss out most of this training, but you might still like to train him to give you the toy in your hand, saving an awful lot of bending down.

If your dog is really keen to retrieve you might occasionally ask him to wait before going to fetch the toy. (Don't ask him to wait every time or he may well decide the game is boring, and stop retrieving altogether.) This is useful for a couple of reasons. It will help him to learn some self-control and it will mean that you can prevent him from running after inappropriate objects like a child's toy or a cricket ball. If you have a dog who is the least bit reluctant to retrieve it is probably best not to ask him to wait.

A word of caution: please make sure that any retrieve toy is suitable for your dog. If you are using a ball for instance, it should be big enough that the dog cannot swallow it or choke on it (but not so big that he can't pick it up). Never be tempted to use a stick to throw for your dog – it can easily stick in the ground and cause damage to your dog's body or mouth if he is still running when he reaches it, or it could stick in the ground when he is returning to you.

Settle

If your puppy understands the words 'settle down' this can be very valuable when he is just in the way, being a bit of a nuisance around the dinner table or when visitors call.

Rather than using a formal stay command, which would imply that he should remain in one place until told to move, settle down is a more relaxed command asking that he just lie down out of the way.

The best approach is to use the words 'settle down' when he just lies down quietly on his own and to reward him for this. It is quite surprising how many owners will spend a large amount of time and effort actively teaching a command, but will ignore the puppy when he does nothing and is just being quiet.

By teaching this at times when your puppy is only too happy to go and have a quiet nap, such as on his return from a walk or after he has had his dinner, you are making a positive association between the words and the action. Once he has made the connection you can put this behaviour on cue and ask for this behaviour when it is required.

Give, mine, drop, thank you!

Dogs need to be taught how to give up to their owners something that they would rather keep. This may be toys, bones, chews, or even that pair of socks they find so tempting. This is not as difficult as it sounds. If we teach our dog that it is worth his while to give things back you will find that he will choose this option.

Stages to giving up a toy:

- Entice your dog to play a tug game, with you at one end of the toy and him at the other. Make sure it is an appropriate toy, e.g. something big enough for you both to get a good hold on, a ball on a rope, raggy or soft toy.

- When you want your dog to give the toy back stop pulling on the toy and stay as still as you can.

- Offer your dog something in exchange for the toy – this may be food or another toy.

- When your dog releases the toy reward him.

- If you are using food as a reward give him the food and offer the toy again for some more playtime.

- If you are using another toy, as soon as he releases the first toy offer to play with him with the second toy.

- The equation in the dogs head should be: play with toy + give up toy = food or another game with a toy.

- Play mix and match games. Sometime your dog will get a food reward for giving up the toy, sometimes he will get another toy and sometimes he gets to play with the same toy.

- It is pure human invention to state that you rather than your dog must end up with the toy. Sometimes using that technique your dog will become more and more possessive over toys. It is much simpler and straightforward for your dog to learn that if he offers to give up his toy the reward is, he gets to keep it.

- As with most dog training we need to put a signal or cue on the behaviour we want to teach our dog.

- Choose a word that you will feel comfortable saying to your dog, some people say 'give', 'drop', 'dead', 'mine' or 'thank you'. It does not matter what you choose as long as you are consistent and repeat the word when your dog releases the toy.

- Using this technique your dog should feel happy and relaxed about giving up the toy.

Exchange is not robbery

Using a similar exchange technique you can teach your dog to relinquish anything including high resource items such as bones or chews.

Teaching your dog from puppyhood that you will exchange whatever he has got for something better will usually prevent any problems from developing. However, if this chance has been missed or your dog has developed a habit of resource guarding you will need a more specialized plan to follow. Please contact a qualified behaviour specialist.

Leave

There will be times when you do not want your dog to chase, eat or perhaps even look at something, in fact you want him to *leave*. The easiest way to go about teaching your dog this skill is to teach him a verbal command that means if you come away from whatever you are doing I will reward you. Follow these simple stages, not moving on to the next stage until your dog understands the previous one.

- Cut up a selection of treats that your dog finds particularly tasty and put them in your pocket or somewhere out of reach of your dog.

- Have a few pieces of less inviting food, perhaps some dried dog biscuit, available as well.
- With the dog off lead (your dog needs to learn how to control himself so it is simpler to start the exercise off lead) place the dried food in front of your dog, but not too close.
- As soon as your dog moves towards the food, remove the food.
- You will have to be very fast, as your dog will naturally try to eat whatever you are placing in front of him.
- Keep repeating this until your dog pauses even for a second, as soon as he pauses say 'good', pick up the dried food and reward him with a treat from the tasty titbits.
- Keep repeating this until you can place the food in front of your dog and your dog does not go for it.
- At this stage your dog has probably been in one particular position, perhaps a down or sit. This means that he has understood not to take the food but only when he is in a particular position, i.e. the one you have practised in.
- Repeat the process with your dog in different positions, down, sit, stand. Also position the food in different places. Start with the floor and then perhaps on your knee or on a chair.
- Your dog needs to understand that *not* taking the food is what reaps the reward.
- When you have reached this stage and not before, start telling your dog what not taking the food is called, i.e. put the cue on the behaviour.
- Choose a simple signal or command such as 'leave'. Do not say no as this is a word he hears constantly and has probably already learnt to ignore.
- Hold the dried food, say 'leave' and place the food in front of your dog. Your dog should now be at the stage where he will leave the food.
- Do not forget to reward your dog every time he leaves the food placed in front of him.

Looking at this from your dog's point of view he will be learning, if I come away from the thing I want I get something even better.

Of course, in the real world where there are fluffy things that need chasing and disgusting things that need eating, humans find it very hard to offer something better. That is why you need to teach 'leave' in different stages until the habit becomes so fixed that your dog will automatically return to you when he hears the word 'leave'.

- Now your dog is at the stage when he can leave dried food in any position, you will need to start making it more difficult. After all, rabbits and pheasants do not sit quietly without moving whilst your dog runs past.
- We now need to start representing the real world.
- Instead of using dried boring food and asking your dog to leave, start to use food that your dog finds more irresistible.
- When your dog is leaving every type of food that you are putting in front of him start to make the food move.
- Ask your dog to leave and roll the food in front of him but not too close.
- Be prepared to put your foot on the food or pick it up quickly if he ignores the command of leave.
- If, however, you are not quick enough and your dog eats the moving food do not worry, just repeat the process making sure that you do not roll the food too close to him.
- When your dog is succeeding and can leave the tasty food, even though it is moving towards him, move on to the next stage.
- Your dog now needs to learn to leave when *he* is moving.
- Place a piece of food on the floor, use the dried food to start with, and walk your dog past the food giving the command of 'leave' if he even looks at the food.
- If he leaves the food or even better, looks at you away from the food, say 'good' and reward him instantly with a high value reward.
- Repeat this process, making it more difficult by replacing the dried food with the tastier food.
- Keep improving on your dog's skill until you can place a row of sausages (or whatever your dog finds irresistible) and call him past them, telling him to leave.
- You are now ready to put his skill to the test in the outside world.
- Practise with food and toys when you are taking him for a walk.
- Ask him to leave something that perhaps you think he has not even seen, such as next door's cat (he has probably smelt it). If he looks at you when you say 'leave' reward him.

Some dogs are more highly motivated by toys than food.

Although food has been used in the above section it is a good idea to work using dog toys instead or as well as food.

Remember to teach in exactly the same way, rewarding your dog with a wonderful game with a special toy if he leaves whatever he has been told to.

Release

Just as important as asking your dog to do something, is to let him know when he has completed the exercise.

Sometimes this is obvious to your dog – you may have asked him to sit and walked away from him. You then call him to you – he will know he has finished the 'sit' because he has been asked to do something else.

But what if you are training your dog to do a longer 'stay'. You ask him to sit and you walk away. You ask your dog to stay. After a period you walk back to your dog and stand beside him. After a few seconds you give your dog the release word and he knows he can stand up.

If he is not used to being 'released' from an exercise he may release himself. You leave him in the sit and walk away; after a few seconds (or longer) he stands up and walks towards you – or maybe just stands up or lays down. He might wait until you are returning to him before he moves. Any of these actions tells you that your dog does not understand when he has finished the exercise. If, however, he knows that another cue or his release word will mark the end he will very soon learn to wait to be released, this saves a lot of misunderstanding and frayed tempers.

Because we cannot tell our dog 'I want you to stay still for one minute' (well, we can, but he won't initially understand what you are talking about) we need to let him know when that time has come. Imagine if someone asks you to watch a stationery person or a place on the wall. You must not move your gaze, you have no idea how long you will have to watch nor is there anything interesting about the object of your attention. It is extremely difficult to do this. If, however, someone asks you to watch the same person/wall and explains that they will tell you when you can stop, the exercise is much easier and you don't feel the need to look around for clues as to whether you can stop watching. The same applies to your dog when he is doing certain exercises.

Introduce the release word to your dog as early in his training as possible, in this way it will quickly become part of the exercise. You may find that when you start teaching your dog to 'sit' he will be lured into the sit, receive his reward and immediately get up. Just before he gets up give him his release word and encourage him to get up, perhaps making an interesting noise, wave your hands around or similar (don't be tempted to drag him by his collar/lead. This will just teach him that his release word means bad news!). So the release word tells your dog 'you've done it, now you can relax until I ask you to do something'.

Choose your release word carefully. You do not want to use a word that might inadvertently finish the exercise. If, for instance, you choose 'OK', this may work while you are in a training situation but what about in everyday behaviour? After all, most of us want our dog to understand how to behave in everyday life, don't we? You might go to answer the door, you ask the dog to sit and stay whilst you go to the door. It's a neighbour asking if you can take a parcel in for him the next day, you say 'OK'. The dog has been released and he wanders out of the door!

If you want to use 'OK' or 'yes' (and a lot of people do use it very successfully) then you must ensure that you say it in a special, excited way, not the way you would use it in everyday conversation. Or you might want to use a word you don't ordinarily use. This serves two purposes, you can get a lot of excitement/praise into the word and also it is a good human word to acknowledge your dog's achievement.

Not quite a release word, but something that will help your dog understand what is required of him is when you are at the field, park or woods (or any safe place where your dog is able to run off lead) when you let your dog off his lead you might say 'go play'. This tells him that he is free to investigate and have a run until you call his name, he doesn't literally have to 'play'! If he always has to wait for this release he is more likely to wait quietly while you take his lead off. This will also help him to understand whether you want him to 'go play' or walk beside you without his lead.

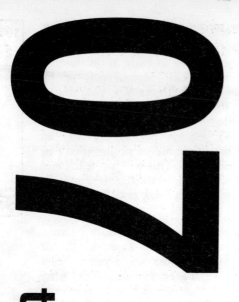

7

top ten tips

In this chapter you will learn:
- how to understand your dog better
- how to read your dog's body language
- how to get the best out of your dog.

1 Managing the environment is the key to stress-free dog ownership

Often the easiest way to solve some common problems is to manage the environment so that our dog cannot perform the behaviour you do not like. Does he raid the bin? Move it out of reach. Does he dig craters in your lawn? Do not allow him unsupervised access to the garden. Housetraining problems? Take him outside more often. Going mad at the door when visitors arrive? Throw a handful of titbits in the kitchen when the doorbell rings and shut the door, only allowing him access to visitors when things have calmed down and your guests are settled. There are hundreds of ways that you can make your life easier and coincidentally, make your dog's life more pleasant just by simply changing a few things.

If your dog pulls on lead all the time, use a suitable head collar or harness. Feed him the best quality food and keep him fit and active, this will save you vet's bills. Make sure your garden is fully dog-proofed, the fence is high enough and there are no holes in the hedges. Check your dog's identity tag regularly, so that if he ever gets lost he can be returned to you quickly.

If your dog barks at the window, shut the door to that room.

If your children leave toys and clothes laying on the floor your puppy will undoubtedly pick them up and run off with them. Don't blame your puppy – teach your children to be tidy!

There will be lots of times when you need your dog to settle down, keep a low profile and not bother you. He'll be much happier and more settled if you give him a large, tasty chew or stuffed Kong to keep him occupied. Likewise, when you have to leave him alone he will be much happier with a tasty chew to keep him busy.

If you have young children and they have friends to play, your dog should be kept apart from the children, or kept under control. He may be fine with your children, but some visiting children may be afraid of dogs and others may get too excited and worry your dog.

Just a little forethought can make things run so much more smoothly.

Practice makes perfect – or does it?

The more practice your dog gets the better he will learn a behaviour. At least 20 times a day ask your pup to come and sit for a pet and a treat or game. The secret of producing a reliably obedient dog lies with numerous, extremely short (less than five seconds) training sessions a day, many times in different locations; indoors, in the garden and out on walks. Get and keep your dog's attention, you may need it in an emergency.

Practise turning your puppy off; tell your pup to settle down at least ten times a day. Practise at home and out on walks, put your dog on lead and establish an early precedent of 'little-quiet-moments' with your puppy. A dog you can take anywhere, pub, shop, friends, is a pleasure to own. Letting your dog act like a delinquent will wear you out. You are what your dog will become.

2 Join a training class

Find your local Association of Pet Dog Trainers' member and join an appropriate class. Most members run classes for dogs of all ages and standards. Training your dog with other like-minded people in a relaxed and stress-free environment is fun and will help you perfect your handling skills and teach your dog good manners around other dogs. Always visit a class first just to observe and make sure that this would be the class for you. All trainers are different and you need to find someone you feel you will get on with.

If you are unable to attend a class, APDT members usually offer one-to-one training which is very effective, although it does not teach your dog how to behave when there are other dogs around. Even just a single one-to-one lesson in your home could be very beneficial. The advantage of a private lesson is that you have the trainer's undivided attention and the training can be personalized to suit you and your dog.

Some dogs get too excited and stressed in a class environment and are much better with one-to-one training. Likewise, some people find a class situation too nerve-wracking and are unable to cope if their puppy is not as quick as the puppy next to them or their puppy continually plays around.

If you are interested in working your dog in any of the many disciplines now available, be it gundog work, obedience, agility, showing, to name a few, you will need good basic obedience first. Dog sports are gaining in popularity all the time and most people started off by taking their dog to a pet dog training class, finding that they really enjoy training their dog and go on to take it more seriously.

Friends, neighbours, even complete strangers are always keen to give you advice on how to train your dog. This advice often tends to be of the 'hit them on the nose with a rolled up newspaper', 'rub his nose in it', 'your dog is being dominant – you must show him who's boss' variety. Please, do not listen to advice from well-meaning amateurs. APDT members have to keep themselves abreast of the latest, scientific, proven methods of training, so always go to a professional for advice.

Dog training is fun

You presumably bought a dog because you love animals and enjoy their company. The best way of building a strong bond with your dog is to spend time training and playing with him. There is no need to set aside extra time for this – you can easily incorporate training into everyday life. Walks are an ideal time to train and play with your dog. It is a very sad sight to see some dogs mooching disconsolately behind their owners on walks, neither paying attention to the other. It is essential that your dog finds you fun to be with on walks and enjoys your company.

If your dog loves to chase toys and bring them back to you, then it is easy to play with him. However, all is not lost if your dog is not interested in toys. Toss some treats or a portion of his daily food allowance over a few square metres of grass and send him to search it out. This will satisfy his hunting instincts and make you much more interesting to be with.

3 Base your relationship with your dog on mutual trust and respect

Your dog should not see you as a dictator but an equal partner. He should look at you for guidance and support without having all his natural enthusiasms curbed. For instance, when your dog is going through his adolescent phase it would be unfair and very frustrating for you if he spends every moment of his walk seeking out other dogs and completely ignoring you. If you work hard on basic obedience, and use good management techniques, it is possible to train your dog to only run off to play with your permission. If you can find another dog owner with a dog of similar age and size (someone from your training class, perhaps) you could meet up for a walk and play session. If you get your dog to sit and look at you, then reward him with a 'go play' cue, then he will learn to seek your permission first. Dogs do deserve a certain amount of freedom to be just dogs. If you have a well-trained dog you will be able to trust him.

You may be told that your breed of dog should never be let off lead, or you may just be terrified that your dog will run away if you allow him any freedom. It is really fair for any dog never to be allowed to run free? It is all down to training a really good recall and your local APDT member could help you with this.

Your relationship with your dog should be a matter of mutual trust and respect not a battle of wills. The only way to achieve this is by training. Trying to impose your will on your dog will not work and will lead to frustration and anger – probably on both sides.

4 Always have a few dog treats in your pocket

Treats make the best reward, as they are quick, easy and effective. The more you reward your dog, especially when teaching a new exercise, the more your dog will want to perform that exercise. It is far, far better to give your dog lots of treats than too few. You never know when an opportunity may arise to reinforce a good behaviour, so be prepared.

Whenever your dog does something good – reward him! A real, positive reward, rather than just 'good dog' will have much more impact on him. When he comes back to you quickly, reward him. Maybe he is walking beautifully beside you on a loose lead – use this opportunity to show him that you really appreciate this. You can use treats in an emergency to distract your dog from things such as fox poo, other dogs, people, joggers, bicycles, etc. If your timing is good you can distract your dog, reward him and pop him back on the lead before he has made the decision to roll in the fox poo, chase the jogger, etc.

If your dog loves his toys best, then carry a small toy with you and use that instead. It is up to you as an owner to know what your dog really loves as a reward and then use it to your advantage.

5 Remember – your dog is not being 'naughty', he is just being a dog

All the behaviours your dog performs that you do not like are normal dog behaviour. Biting, barking, hunting, fighting, weeing, pooing, jumping up, playing, stealing food, chewing, all these behaviours are normal to your dog. Because of the fact that dogs now live as part of a family, we have to educate them about how, when or whether at all to behave like dogs!

It is most unfair to get cross with your dog for being a dog. It is our job to teach them how they can best live alongside us to our mutual benefit.

Puppy play biting needs to be inhibited in a systematic manner so that if, in later life, your dog is ever put in a position where he has no alternative but to bite, he does not bite with the full force of his jaws. See the section in Chapter 05 on bite inhibition.

Excessive barking needs to be managed and controlled so that dogs do not cause a nuisance to others.

We need to teach our dogs to enjoy our company and intervene quickly if they show signs of wanting to run after game and other livestock. A dog should never be off lead where there are sheep or cattle around. A farmer has every right to shoot a dog he believes is worrying his livestock. Always be sensible and if in doubt keep your dog on a lead.

Early socialization with other dogs, adults and children and carefully controlled play with other puppies and dogs should ensure that your dog does not get involved in fights with other dogs. On the rare occasions that this does occur, if a puppy has been taught good bite inhibition, no serious harm should occur.

Puppies and rescue dogs need painstaking house-training. This does not happen by itself, you need to make sure your puppy is given the opportunity to go outside often enough and rewarded when he does. Do not punish him if he has an accident indoors, that is your fault not his as you were not watching him closely enough.

Your dog's character traits and his behaviour will often be closely linked to his breed. Border collies herd, retrievers carry things around in their mouth, hounds follow scent hunting, terriers go down holes after rats and rabbits, guarding breeds bark at strangers, fighting breeds play roughly, lapdogs can't go for ten-mile hikes. You can with careful training modify and redirect your dog's behaviour, but you cannot extinguish it completely.

Remember, we are the ones with brainpower. If you attempt to change your dog's behaviour by using force and coercion you will destroy your relationship and may actually encourage your dog to return force with force and have a deep mistrust of people. Apply your brain to solving problems with help from experts if necessary.

6 Crate train your puppy

If you are thinking of getting a puppy or already have a young dog, a properly used crate is a wonderful tool. Older dogs can also be crate-trained if necessary. As far as a puppy is concerned a crate is simply a den, a comfortable safe place to retire to for a sleep and a bolt hole if life gets too much. Of course, your puppy should not be left in a crate all day, that is misuse of the crate.

There is a conception amongst the general public that it is somehow cruel to shut a puppy in a crate, but a puppy does not see it like that. Occasionally, some puppies cannot settle in a cage and obviously it would be cruel to insist if they are very distressed. Some puppies are very unhappy when they are first left alone at night, and sometimes it is worth taking the crate and your puppy into your bedroom, or alternatively you could sleep downstairs, for the first few nights.

The vast majority of puppies will not soil in their crate. This can be of immense help when house-training, as you can take your puppy straight outside when he wakes from a nap. If you allow him to fall asleep anywhere he will probably move and relieve himself as soon as he wakes up, wherever that may be; if he has been crated he will whine to get out to go and relieve himself. If you cannot supervise your puppy, then pop him in his crate.

The crate is a safe place for your puppy to go when you are out, when you have visitors and when you are vacuuming or washing the kitchen floor.

If you go away to visit friends or take your puppy on holiday, his crate will provide a safe, portable home and he will not cause you embarrassment if he has an accident, so you and your puppy will be welcome anywhere.

It is advisable to keep your puppy crated until he is past the chewing stage. You may have to buy a larger crate, but it will be worth it. If your dog ever injures himself or has an operation that necessitates rest, it will be extremely useful to be able to keep him in his crate. Trying to rest a dog is virtually impossible if they can charge around the house.

You can now buy soft, light, collapsible tent-like crates for your dog, which are very portable and immensely useful.

If you have an estate car, then a crate in the back keeps your dog comfortable and safely confined. It also leaves room around the crate for luggage, shopping, etc. Incidentally, all dogs should be confined in some way in the car. A loose dog is very dangerous in an accident and many people have been injured, sometimes fatally, by flying dogs (let alone the injuries caused to dogs). An unrestrained dog in the back seat is in as much danger as a child who has not been belted in. A crate, a good dog guard, or a dog car harness are essential if you have your dog in the car with you. If you own one of the herding breeds that are inclined to bark when cars are whizzing past, then a crate with a blanket over can block out the view and put a stop to this particular behaviour.

7 Learn as much as you can about dog behaviour

If you are interested enough to read this book, you might like to learn more about dog behaviour and training. A good start would be a subscription to one of the monthly magazines published for dog owners. These are readily available at your local newsagent and are packed full of articles on dog behaviour, training and health as well as all the latest news concerning dogs.

Your local library should have a good selection of books on dogs. From reading this book you will understand how kind, fair and effective training works and how you can teach your dog to be an obedient, happy family pet without using force or confrontation. Not all books adhere to these principles; many still advocate coercive methods, the use of check/choke chains and other unnecessary equipment. When you read books, do not assume that because 'experts' write them that they will give you the best, most up-to-date advice. However, with a discerning mind it can be fascinating to read some of the more old-fashioned books.

There is a wealth of good books and videos available. Look at the recommended reading list in Chapter 14.

Observing other dogs and their owners can also teach you a lot. Compare a happy, carefree, obedient dog with an out of control hooligan. How do the owners behave? Do they appear confident or unsure? Are they constantly nagging their dogs? Do they play with their dogs? Studying the behaviour of owners and their dogs can be a real eye opener, and it is always easier to see where someone else may be going wrong than to see your own mistakes.

8 Learn to read your dog's body language

It may sound obvious, but dogs do not communicate with words. They do not speak English or any other verbal language. They communicate using subtle body language and it can help our relationship with them enormously if we take a little time to learn what dog language means. We try very hard to teach them some of our words and so it would be nice if we could understand what they were trying to tell us. Dogs use their whole bodies, mouth, eyes, ears, tail and posture, to convey their feelings, both physical and mental, and more and more research into this fascinating subject is going on all the time. There have been some great books published on this subject. (Look at the recommended reading list in Chapter 14.)

Because dogs come in such a huge variety of shapes and sizes, it can be more difficult to read the signals of some breeds. Tail docking is a good example. It can be very hard, if not impossible, to work out what a docked dog's tail is telling you.

What follows is a very brief description of the most common body language you may observe in your dog.

The mouth
A dog's mouth can be very expressive, and convey all the emotions he is feeling at that moment. If you pick up on the signals your puppy gives you early enough you can defuse a great deal of the behaviour about to be shown.

Mouth open

Mouth relaxed and slightly open, tongue may be visible. The sign of a happy, contented dog.

Mouth closed

A tightly closed mouth accompanied by a turning away of the head means 'I'm a bit unsure' and is a pacifying gesture. A closed mouth with a slight forward lean of the ears and head and a forward gaze means 'I'm watching something of interest over there'. Standing very still with a closed mouth and ears erect means 'I am listening to something'. It is a bit like when we stand still to decide what to do next.

Lips

Lips curled to expose some teeth means 'Don't come any closer'. This is a threat, often used after more subtle signals have been used and failed. It usually works extremely well at getting other dogs and humans to move away.

Lips curled to expose major teeth, mouth partly open and nose area wrinkled is the threat that means, 'I mean it, if you do not go away I will bite you'. Lips curled to expose all the teeth and gums above the front teeth with very noticeable wrinkles above the nose, 'This is your last chance, if you don't back off I really will bite'.

Fig 15 Various dog's mouth expressions

Grinning

There are certain breeds of dogs that 'smile' and it can be a 'submissive' gesture used when you are greeted by your dog. Many people mistake a 'smile' for an aggressive display and nothing could be further from the truth. Dalmations, Dobermans and many terriers all are know to be 'smilers'.

Eyes

Eye contact

Dogs do not naturally view direct eye contact as a pleasant experience. In the wild they would view a direct stare as a threat. However, a puppy will soon learn that eye contact combined with a pleasant facial expression from the owner and a titbit it a very rewarding experience. This is something that should be trained from puppyhood, as children are all prone to look a dog in the eye. Liking eye contact can also make a nervous dog a bit more confident. Never stare your dog down in anger, as this will make him very wary of eye contact with anyone else.

Staring

A direct stare at another dog is often a threat. It often happens in a training class situation that two dogs will stare at each other and if this is not interrupted by distracting them and turning their heads away, it will usually lead to trouble. Off lead you will often see two dogs standing, staring at each other. Usually one dog will back down by turning his head away.

Showing the whites of the eye

Usually a very fearful dog that will bite because of the position he is in.

Enlarged pupils

A dog in a highly aroused state will have dilated pupils.

The tail

We have all probably heard people say 'He didn't mean it, he was wagging his tail!' There are many different ways of wagging a tail and they all signify different things.

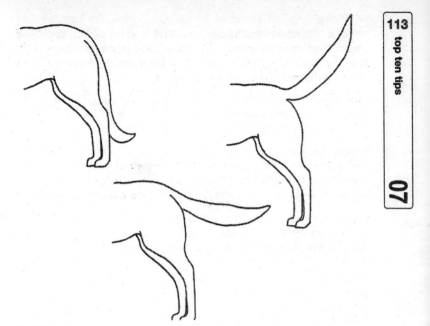

Fig 16 Various dog's tail wagging expressions

9 Make it your dog's responsibility to stay in touch with you on walks

Very few dogs will stay in sight all the time on walks. They get their noses down on wonderful scents and disappear into the undergrowth; they will chase rabbits, squirrels, pheasants and sometimes deer. They go and say hello to every other dog and human that they meet. Most owners panic immediately their dog goes out of sight and quickly call them back, usually with no response. They then keep on calling until the dog eventually returns from his adventures, tired but happy with their run.

This means that all the time your dog is away he is secure in the knowledge that you are close by and will wait for his return. Of course, if you get angry and punish your dog when he returns your recall will get even slower as your dog learns that coming back is not a pleasant experience.

Your dog needs to be a bit worried that he might lose you on a walk, not the other way around. If you are unpredictable and keep your dog on his toes he will return more quickly. When your dog runs off ahead of you along a path, try turning and going in the opposite direction without a word. When your dog comes bounding up to you, praise him and give him a treat. You can also hide from your dog when he is not looking, keeping quiet so that he comes looking for you.

This is best done when your puppy is a youngster and still unsure of himself. However, it will also work with older dogs if you take them to an unfamiliar place and play the hiding game.

If you constantly tell your dog where you are he knows that he can carry on with whatever is occupying him safe in the knowledge that you are waiting for him. On familiar territory he may also know his way home, or where the car is parked.

You could also have a problem getting your dog back if you are too free and easy with the rewards. Dogs work better if they don't know what good things will come their way when they come back to you. If your dog knows what a recall means, reward the fastest, quickest responses or play a game with him when he is extra quick at coming back. If you reward him when he comes back to you even if he has taken ten minutes then that is what you are training.

10 Reward, Reward, Reward!

We often ignore dogs when they are being good because they are not bothering us, but we are missing golden opportunities to teach our dogs some important lessons. We are also minimizing the chances of him doing something we don't want him to just to gain your attention.

If your dog is lying quietly while you are busy pop him a treat when you walk past him, telling him 'good boy' quietly. When visitors call, your dog can be sitting quietly but he is ignored, he then jumps up to say hello, and hey presto! He has the attention he wants. If it is a puppy you have, get your visitors to bend down to his level to say hello so he will not have a chance to learn to jump for a greeting. If you have a really small puppy and your visitor finds it difficult to bend down then hold your pup in your arms for your visitors to greet.

When your puppy greets a dog nicely and quietly and is calm around other dogs, praise and reward him. Don't just take it for granted that your dog knows how to have manners around other dogs because he does not. If he plays with rough dogs he learns to play rough and some dogs just cannot cope with this type of play so reinforce all the nice behaviour around other dogs.

When you are eating your meals and your puppy is lying quietly, before he learns the art of begging at the table go over to where he is lying down and praise him quietly.

If you are standing talking to a friend and your dog is sitting quietly by your side then keep slipping him titbits without saying anything to him, carry on your conversation and your puppy will learn to sit and let you get on with what you need to do while he is a shining example of how a dog should be taught to behave.

Any chance that you have reward and reward again.

08

clicker training

In this chapter you will learn:
- the history of clicker training
- how to start with the clicker
- what you can do with the clicker.

The history of the clicker

Reward-based, motivational training has been around for many years but training was still compulsive. For example, the dog was physically made to sit and then rewarded. Gradually we have seen a change to a much more gentle, fun and effective way of obtaining the behaviours we want from our dogs. While the training method in this book has concentrated on those gentle, fun and effective methods, i.e the food lure/reward method, we cannot ignore the emergence of the clicker in dog training that has happened over the last few years.

Many training instructors now run their training classes exclusively using clickers to help owners train their dogs. Each owner is provided with a clicker and when the dog has done something right, he is clicked and rewarded. (Refer to the following section on clicker training.)

Although clicker training is a comparatively new concept in dog training, it has been used for many years in training other types of animal. As far back as the 1930s, animal behaviour experts were experimenting with clickers, know then as 'crickts', and in 1951 Professor B. F. Skinner produced a paper, *How to Teach Animals*, where he described the use of a clicker. From the 1940s to the present day the clicker has been used to train many types of animals including 140 species of birds, dolphins, horses and a bull!

However, it wasn't until the 1980s that Karen Pryor, who started using a clicker while training marine mammals, introduced the clicker to dog trainers. In her revolutionary book *Don't Shoot the Dog* she describes how the clicker can help train anything, from people to dogs. Since then there have been many books and videos on how to use a clicker for training your dog. With correct instructions, you too can train your dog using a clicker. For more information, refer to Chapter 14.

An introduction to clicker training

Clicker training is one of the most modern, effective and enjoyable methods available. Based on sound scientific principles, this tool will allow you to communicate with your dog – and train him to do practically any action you choose.

What is a clicker?

A clicker is a small plastic box containing a piece of flexible steel. When pressed at one end, it makes a distinctive 'click, click' sound that can be taught to have meaning to your dog.

How does it work?

After a few repetitions, your dog learns that the sound of the clicker means he's done the right thing and that a reward – food, play or affection, is on its way.

How will my dog understand what it means?

Your dog will make the association between the clicker and goodies by repetition and reward. The sound of the clicker marks the dog's action as being right, a little like putting a tick next to a correct sum on a page!

Why is the clicker so effective?

It is always positive and highly accurate. You can give clear information to your dog about his actions up close, or from a distance, without your feelings about your stressful day or the weather being expressed, as they often are in your voice! The clicker rewards actions you like – simply ignore actions that you don't.

How do I start?

Make sure you and your dog are somewhere calm and quiet, such as your lounge or the garden. Have some really tasty, small treats, such as cheese, sausage or chicken at the ready. Hold the clicker behind your back to begin with – there is no need to point it at your dog, and you should avoid clicking too near his ears!

- Say your dog's name in a happy voice.
- As soon as he looks at you, click and give a reward.
- Repeat this three or four times.
- Soon, your dog will start to understand the meaning of the clicker and will react to the sound, thinking, 'Great, where's my treat?'

You will also have taught him to pay attention to you when you say his name! Now you are ready to move on to other exercises and tasks!

Sit

- Keep quiet, and show your dog you have a food treat in your hand. Put it on his nose, right up close. Now lift your hand up and back, so he has to look right up to follow your fingers. The movement of him looking upwards like this causes a physical chain reaction – his rear end has to go down.

- Suddenly your dog is sitting! As soon as his bottom hits the ground, click, and then give your dog the treat.

- Repeat this a few times. (If your dog's front legs come off the ground, your hand is probably too high.)

- Now you can say the word 'sit' just before you move the food lure. In a matter of minutes you have taught your dog a verbal request to sit, plus a really effective hand signal. Congratulations!

- Now, you need to phase out the food lure. With no food in your hand, ask your dog to sit. If he does so, click immediately, then give a food treat. If your dog does not sit when asked, help him with the hand signal, then reward for good efforts.

- Practise until your dog's sits are really quick and totally reliable by asking your dog to sit before he gets anything in life he likes – having his dinner, having his lead put on, being let out into the garden – it's his way of saying please and thank you.

09

where to find a puppy

In this chapter you will learn:
- what to look for when choosing a breeder
- what to look for when choosing a puppy
- the places to avoid.

Deciding on getting a puppy is a big step to take especially if this is your first puppy. Amongst other things, you should take into account the time you can devote to your pup, how to train him, the size of dog that will suit your home and car, the grooming requirements, how much exercise he will need, whether to get a male or female, the cost of food, equipment, veterinary treatment and boarding kennels, and particularly consider a breed that will suit your lifestyle. If you decide on a pedigree puppy, you are fairly sure of knowing what you are getting; you'll know how big he will be, how long the coat will be, the breed's characteristics, how much exercise he will need, and how much it will cost you to feed him. With a crossbreed or mongrel you may have no idea of his eventual size, what his coat will look like, or whether he will show any breed charactistics that have been passed down from his parents.

Where to start

If you decide on acquiring a puppy and having decided on the breed that all the family have agreed upon, a good starting point is to contact the breed club. All breeds registered with the Kennel Club have breed clubs. They can provide useful information about the characteristics of the breed and what is required for its general care and welfare. They may also be able to put you in touch with breeders in your part of the country. See Chapter 14 for contact details of the Kennel Club.

You can visit Discover Dogs, which is held at Earls Court, London every November and at Crufts, held every March at the NEC, Birmingham. Here you will be able to see 180 different breeds registered with the Kennel Club. You'll be able to speak to owners and breeders who can tell you all there is to know about the breed(s) you may be considering, both the good and not so good points. They should be able to give you a contact of someone who has bought a puppy from them so you can find out what the breed is like to live with.

Whether you are looking for a pedigree pup, a crossbreed or a mongrel, finding the right puppy that has been reared correctly and has started socialization is essential. It may take some time to find a good breeder who rears puppies in 'ideal' conditions and has a litter for sale, so be patient. When you consider that you will have your puppy for at least ten years it is well worth getting it right. Try to see as many litters as possible and as many breeders as possible. If you arrange to visit a number of breeders there is less risk of falling in love with the first puppy you see!

Re-homing centres

Sometimes unwanted litters are left at re-homing centres. National re-homing centres are the RSPCA, the Dogs Trust and the Blue Cross. Other well-known re-homing centres are the Dogs Home Battersea and Wood Green Animal Shelter. Please refer to Chapter 14 on 'Taking it further'. There are also many independently-run re-homing centres, many of which have charitable status.

What to look for

You may not be able to see the sire but it is *essential* that you see the dam with her pups. If the breeder gives an excuse as to why the dam is not available, she's being taken for a walk for example, walk away! When you do see the dam watch her temperament while she is on her own with the pups and when you pick up one of her pups. If she appears stressed or shows any sign of aggression, move on to the next breeder on your list. Any signs of aggression from the dam can be passed on to the pups.

Ask questions about the parents. How old are the dam and sire? Neither should be any younger than one year old. Has the dam previously had a litter? If so, when was it? Bitches should not be bred from on consecutive seasons.

Ideally the pups should be reared in the home so they can become accustomed to the sights, sound and smells of everyday household appliances and the hustle and bustle of people coming and going. This will make life much easier when the pup makes the transition from the breeder to his new home. If the pup is reared in a kennel outside he won't get the necessary benefits of socialization and the stimulation that a puppy reared in the home will have. Even if the puppies are kept in kennels they should be allowed some time in the home during the day so they become accustomed to household noises, so ask how often the puppies are allowed indoors and how much time the breeder and other people spend with the pups. Puppies that are devoid of human contact at this stage of their life may be shy of people later on. If the puppy is reared in a kennel, make sure it is dry, warm and clean, and is in a good state of repair.

There should be plenty of toys for the puppies to play with that will help stimulate them and help them develop mentally and physically. Also watch how the pups play and interact with each other as well as the dam. This is a very important part of how puppies learn to behave as dogs.

If possible go and see a litter at three weeks of age when their eyes and ears open and they start moving around, then each week or two weeks until they are allowed to come home. During this time, the breeder should start socializing them with as many different experiences as is sensibly possible, starting with gently handling at just a few days of age. This will cause mild stress, which will help the pup deal with more stressful situations later in life. The breeder should play an important part in starting the socialization process that will help the pup cope with life when he goes to his new home. Apart from handling the pups, the breeder should ensure they meet as many different people of all ages as is possible. For example, if the breeder is a lady make sure she has invited men to handle the pups and also children of different ages. The puppies can even be taken out in the car for short journeys.

Hereditary ailments

If you are buying a pedigree puppy, you should be aware of the hereditary ailments of your chosen breed. Check that the sire and dam have been tested for those ailments by asking to see the veterinarian's certificate. Ideally, the breeder should also have the certificates of previous generations. This will not guarantee the pup won't develop the ailments later in life but it reduces the risk. Some hereditary ailments, deafness and Collie Eye Anomaly (CEA) for example can be tested for in pups when they are six or seven weeks old, so make sure this has been down. Ask the ages of the sire and dam. Many hereditary ailments may not show for 12 months; others won't show until the dog is two years or even older, so dogs should not be bred from any younger than one year old. Many medium size and large breeds can suffer from a hereditary ailment called hip dysplasia, the parents and past generations should have been 'hip scored'. Each breed who suffers from this ailment has an average hip score so when doing your research into breeds you like, check if they suffer from hip dysplasia and find out what the average hip score is for that breed, and then ask the breeder to see the hip scores. The scores range from 0 to 100; the lower the score, the better the hips.

Breeding and Sale of Dogs Act

Under the Breeding and Sale of Dogs Act anyone who breeds more than five litters a year must be licensed by the Local Authority. The premises are inspected annually by an independent vet so if the breeder you intend to buy a puppy from breeds more than five litters a year, ask to see the licence. As well as other restrictions, this bans the mating of bitches under 12 months of age and on consecutive seasons. It also bans the sale of pups under the age of eight weeks.

What age to buy?

If the breeder is not licensed they can sell puppies younger than eight weeks of age but there is a fine line between the essential learning period when the puppy learns how to behave like a dog by playing and interacting with its siblings and dam, and going to a new home. Buy a puppy that is too young and it will miss out on those early learning benefits that only his mother could teach him and by playing with his litter mates. Buy one that's too old and it will miss out on the 'critical' socialization period. This is between four and about 14 weeks of age.

The dam should have been fed on a good quality, nutritious diet before, during pregnancy and while lactating. This will give the pups a good, healthy start to life. Also ask what the pups have been fed during weaning and what solid food they are fed on now. The breeder should give you a diet sheet when you collect your puppy, usually with a small bag of their present diet. If you intend to change your puppy's diet then give your puppy a few weeks to settle into his new home first, as too many changes all at once may stress your puppy resulting in a severe bout of diarrhoea, and then change his diet gradually over a few days. For example, feed 75 per cent of the original diet and 25 per cent of the new diet, the next day feed 50 per cent of the original diet and 50 per cent of the new diet. The next day feed 25 per cent of the original diet and 75 per cent of the new diet, until finally you feed 100 per cent of the new diet.

Check out the puppy

Check out the pups to ensure they don't have any discharge from eyes, nose, ears and the rear end. Their skin should not be dry or flaky and their coats should be clean. Make sure the puppies and dam have been wormed and that the dam and sire are up to date with their inoculations. Worming puppies should start when they are four weeks of age and thereafter every two weeks until 12 weeks of age. An overly fat puppy tummy and smelly breath is a sign that your chosen puppy could be infested with worms.

If buying a Kennel Club registered puppy, when you collect him, expect to go home with a receipt of purchase, the pup's Pedigree, a diet sheet, some food and an insurance that covers your pup's health for six months. If the puppy is a specific breed but the parents are not Kennel Club registered, you won't be able to register him but it would be reasonable to pay less for him.

Me, me, me!

You may find when viewing a litter of puppies that one or two will appear to be saying 'take me, take me' as they crawl all over you. On the other hand, there may be one or two that are squeezed into a corner not wanting to interact with you or indeed, the other puppies.

At about four weeks of age when the puppies' senses are all functioning and they are able to move around they will start to play with each other and with their mother. They will start to learn through play, amongst other things, bite inhibition and dominance and submissive behaviours to their litter mates and their mother. The more dominant puppies are likely to be the ones that 'choose' you. The puppies that have a stronger character may prove to be difficult for a first-time owner. They may be more difficult to train and take more liberties at home. That does not mean the puppy is 'dominant' over humans – dogs are not dominant over humans (see the recommended reading list in Chapter 14). If he has been the bully of the litter, he may be a bully with other dogs later on. Alternatively, the shy puppy which is usually the one that the dominant puppies have 'picked on' may appear scared of the outside world and everything he meets in it. As a general rule if you are looking for a pet or companion dog, find a puppy with a temperament somewhere between the two extremes.

However, the temperament you see as a puppy is not necessarily the temperament you will get when he is an adult. There are many things that can change a dog's character. For example, a dog with a bold character will become less bold, even introvert, if he is not socialized at the right time and in the right way; or if an inappropriate, harsh method of training is used; if he's abused physically or psychologically by his owner or a member of the family; he has cold, damp living conditions; he is fed an inappropriate diet; he is attacked by another dog or is exposed to lengthy periods of an unpleasant stimulus such as loud noises, fireworks, bird scarers, or gun shots for example. In fact, there are a multitude of possibilities that will change a bold dog in to a scared dog. Conversely, a puppy that is an introvert can become an extrovert if he is socialized in the right way and at the right time; he is trained using positive, motivational methods, and his general living conditions and treatment by the family are all positive. If his early learning experiences with you are rewarding ones and he has many good interactions with people and dogs in particular, his personality and confidence will grow.

Questions to ask

As well as being prepared with all the questions you will need to ask the breeder, you also need to be prepared for the breeder to ask you a lot of questions. A good breeder will care where the puppies are going and may ask some rather searching questions. For example, they might want to know how long the puppy will be left on his own; where he will sleep; whether you have had a dog before; whether you are prepared to train the puppy; whether you have children and if so how many and what ages; the size of your garden and whether it's enclosed; why you chose that specific breed and whether you have studied the breed characteristics, and whether you intend to breed from him.

Male or female

More often than not, when it comes down to deciding on a male or female, it usually boils down to personal preference. Some people on the other hand just don't care as long as they get a puppy! Dogs have a very acute sense of smell, so an adolescent or adult male will detect the scent of a bitch in season from some distance away. This may have the effect of the dog not eating and loss of toilet training. Some males will go to any length to get to the source of the scent so the owners must take precautions and ensure their dog cannot escape from the garden. Neutering, of course, will permanently solve the 'problem'.

Some people prefer bitches as they are smaller than the male of the breed and people believe that bitches are more compliant and easier to train. Compliance and trainability depends very much on breed characteristics and how you have socialized the puppy and the method you use to train the puppy. Bitches usually come into season twice a year and the first season can start as young as six months of age. A season will last about 18 days during which time the vulva swells from where there is a bloody discharge. Mid way through the oestrus the bitch will be receptive to a male dog and may be as intent to get to a male as a male is in getting to her! They can have phantom pregnancies after their season has finished where they may collect toys and may guard them. Some bitches go as far as producing milk during a phantom pregnancy. A bitch's personality may also change when she is coming up to a season and she may go off her food, become snappy and irritable with other dogs or she may become quieter and retreat to her bed wanting to be left alone.

Both males and females can suffer from medical problems later in life if they are not neutered, including different types of cancers for both dog and bitch, and a potentially life-threatening infection called Pyometra in bitches which is not always detectable until it is too late.

If you already have a dog at home and you are looking for a second, then the best match are dogs of the opposite gender. So if you have a male, the best choice to make when looking for a puppy is a female. Although you must ensure that one, or both, are neutered at the right age.

To work or not to work

There are many breeds of dog that are classified as a working dog; Border collies, retrievers and spaniels to name but three. Most working breeds have two bloodlines, one for the working dog and the other for the show dog. A dog bred to perform a job of work will have been bred for the specific behaviours that give him the ability to work and will come from generations of working dogs. The dog bred for the show ring will have been bred for his looks and will come from generations of show dogs. While show dogs still retain their working instincts, generally they have been somewhat diluted by the generations of breeding for looks rather than their working ability. If you are looking for a pet or companion dog, find a breeder that breeds for the show ring so the dog has less of the working instinct. If you buy a puppy that has come from generations of dogs bred to work, then you are likely to end up with a dog that has the desire to work which you may not be able to satisfy.

Double trouble

Even if you are an experienced owner or trainer, do not be persuaded or tempted to buy two pups from the same litter. Looking after and training one puppy can be difficult enough, but with two will be twice as difficult. If the pups are from the same litter, the bond between them can be very strong to the point where they cannot bear to be parted from each other and in many cases getting them to pay attention to you may be very difficult indeed.

Buying a crossbreed

You may of course prefer to buy a dog that is not a pedigree. Many breeders advertise litters for sale in local newspapers or advertise in veterinary surgeries. Just because the dog is not a pedigree does not mean the breeder should take any less care over rearing the puppies; you should still insist on seeing the dam. Apart from hereditary ailments, you should still ask pertinent questions.

Places to avoid

Puppy farms

There are unfortunately unscrupulous breeders who prey on people's sympathies and sell puppies that have been raised in less than ideal conditions. Puppy farms have had bad publicity and rightly so. These are establishments that breed from a bitch every time she comes into season until she is physically and mentally worn out. When you go to see a puppy, that's usually all you will see; just one puppy. You won't be able to make a choice from a litter and you won't be able to see the dam. The mental and physical health of the puppies is usually suspect, as they will probably be covered in fleas, unlikely to have been wormed and have had no socialization. A puppy like this will tug on your heartstrings but given that the pup has had a really bad start in life, you may find yourself with a sickly, nervous puppy that will grow up to be a sickly, nervous dog.

Pet shops

Pet shops may obtain puppies from puppy farms or breeders who have a surplus of puppies. Either way you won't know at what age the pups were taken away from their mother. There is a great risk of the pups not being in the best of health, they may not have been wormed regularly, if at all, and are unlikely to have been socialized.

Local newspapers

Puppies are often advertised for sale in local newspapers. Some of them may be genuine but others may not. The advertisements to be suspicious of are those that offer many different breeds of puppy for sale. These may be puppy farms or they may be a dealer who has bought unwanted pups from different sources. The dealer may offer to bring the puppy to your home or meet you somewhere convenient. If that is the case then do not buy! If you answer an advertisement in a local newspaper and the 'breeder' offers to meet you with the puppy or even bring him to your house, just say 'thanks, but no thanks'. This is someone with something to hide; a dealer, puppy farm, or someone who has bought an entire litter with the sole aim of making a profit.

10

where to find an older dog

In this chapter you will learn:
- where to find an older dog
- where to find rescue centres
- about specific breed rescue.

You may of course decide on getting an older dog that has been through the puppy stage, is house trained and has grown out of all the puppy behaviours that some people find difficult to deal with. Probably the most usual places to find an older dog is at National re-homing centres such as the RSPCA, The Dogs Trust and The Blue Cross. Other well known re-homing centres are the Dogs Home Battersea and Wood Green Animal Shelter. Please refer to Taking it further. There are also many independently run re-homing centres, many of which have charitable status.

Re-homing centres

Most re-homing centres will ask for payment. This may be a standard charge or a sliding scale depending on the age of the dog. The dog will usually be neutered before he leaves the centre. When acquiring a dog from one of the nationally recognized re-homing centres, expect a lengthy question and answer session so the centre can be fairly sure the dog is going to a good home and the family and dog are well suited. Before being allowed to take your chosen dog home, expect a home visit from one of their representatives. This visit will give the centre more of an insight as to where the dog will be going, to ask questions about the family and their routines, and make sure there is nothing that might pose a problem for the dog or the family, such as another dog or cat in residence and that the garden is secure. It will also give you the opportunity to ask questions of the representative that you may have forgotten to ask when you visited the centre. A few weeks after you have had the dog a representative from the centre may pay another visit to your home. The purpose of this visit is to make sure the dog is being well looked after, that the owners have not found any unexpected problems with the dog and to talk about how the dog has settled in and adapted to the family's routine.

An independent re-homing centre will still make a charge for the dog but depending on how far away the new potential owners live, may not be able to make home visits. Depending on financial constraints, they may not be able to neuter the dog either.

Breed rescue societies

Most breeds of dogs have their own rescue societies which take in a specific breed of dog for re-homing. When an owner of a specific breed feels they can no longer keep the dog, instead of handing it over to a national or independent re-homing centre, they may choose to hand it over to a breed rescue society. Some of these societies have contacts throughout the country and others are relatively small and work within a comparatively small area.

When a dog is handed in, the owner hands over ownership of the dog to the breed rescue society and they will then find the dog a suitable home. The original owner will have no further contact with the dog. Depending on the size of the society and the number of volunteers it has, you may or may not get a home visit.

Because the breed rescue societies often take in dogs that have been Kennel Club registered, the registration papers are kept by the society or returned to the breeder. This is to prevent new owners breeding from their new dog and selling Kennel Club registered puppies.

All the breed re-homing centres are published in the 'Dog Rescue Directory' produced by the Kennel Club. They will send a copy free of charge.

11

common problems

In this chapter you will learn:
- how to stop your dog jumping up
- how to teach your puppy not to bark
- how to curb attention-seeking behaviour.

Of course, bringing up a puppy is not all plain sailing and you should always be prepared for when things start to go wrong.

Jumping up

Why do they do it?

If you have ever watched a young puppy greeting an older dog for the first time he will, if he is sensible, approach steadily and give a hello sniff, then he wiggles up to the dog's mouth and tries to lick his muzzle. This will tell the older dog that he knows his place and wants to be friends.

As small puppies, of course, many people encourage this behaviour as firstly it is a cute puppy and secondly it is a long way to bend down. As the puppy grows and the jumping up becomes more enthusiastic it becomes a bit of a nuisance. Also this will have now extended to all your friends and maybe even total strangers in the street that he would like to be his friend.

It is therefore very unfair to use punitive methods to correct this behaviour. If you were trying your best to show how much you wanted someone to be your friend and they smacked you on the nose with a newspaper or stood on your toes I think it can be guaranteed that it would hurt your feelings more than your person.

From very early on it is a good idea to show the puppy what is acceptable as a greeting from a human perspective, of course teaching him to shake hands is an option, but it is much better to use something more appropriate such as sit and look pretty.

Start by using members of your own family as these are the people who he meets regularly and on whom he can practise his skills; also you will have control over the reaction of the people he greets. Holding the puppy on a short lead, and with a treat in your hand, stand still as the person approaches. When your puppy jumps ask the approaching person to also stand still, when the puppy stops jumping give him a treat and get the other person to walk away and re-approach. Once the puppy is sitting automatically when approached you can then ask for a sit and reward. Practise this on every family member, starting with adults and work down to the children. You should then use friends as guinea pigs and get the puppy to practise on a range of people until this becomes second nature.

The real problem is around young children who are quick, loud and fun. Do not let your puppy play chasing games with children, but give them quiet training games to play. If your puppy learns that such games with children are a no-no then he won't be jumping at children he meets in the park.

It is not a good idea to get other people to give your dog treats when they approach or he will expect every person he meets to feed him and this will actually increase his desire to run up to other people and jump on them for treats.

Resource guarding

It can be funny to see a tiny puppy standing over his food bowl and guarding it from all comers. Who does he think he is? Of course, if this behaviour carries on you may have major problems when he is an adult. It is not so funny when your dog is guarding the kitchen because he has a biscuit on the floor and will not allow anyone in until he has eaten it.

From day one, many owners start by taking the puppy's dinner away and then giving it back to him. This will show the pup that you do not mean to deprive him of this forever and if this is done before any growling behaviour has happened he will not look on you as a threat.

In the puppy's eyes, however, this does mean that you approaching his food bowl could mean the loss of his dinner, and if he has been successful in keeping people away in the past by growling and this is now not working, then snapping may be the next course of action. Think how you would feel if after a hard day's work you were presented with a nice hot dinner only to have someone snatch it away just to prove to you that they could. No one, however, feels threatened when in a restaurant the waiter approaches you with a serving dish to offer more vegetables or another helping of chips.

When a problem has already established itself, in order to ensure that your approach is welcomed, start by putting a small amount of food in his bowl. If he is fed on meat and biscuits then the biscuit content goes in first as this is not so valuable. Once he has started eating, approach and place a very small amount of the meat content in the bowl. If you repeat adding the meat until he has finished his dinner he will soon welcome you coming near his bowl as you are adding nice tasty things and not removing anything. Once the adults in the house can do this then the children can take a turn. It is important that the puppy learns how he should behave when he has food. If you tell the children not to go near the dog when he is eating this means that you must ensure that all visitors and their children know the same rules. It is not possible to ensure that no one approaches when your dog has food as it may be that you do not know that a tasty morsel has been hidden in his bed when you go to stroke him, or that the spot in the garden where you are standing is where a tasty bone has been buried.

Another option is to feed the dog from several bowls instead of just one. Sometimes the seeds of food guarding behaviour can be sown unwittingly by the breeder who feeds a whole litter from just one or two bowls. Puppies soon learn to get in early and guard their portion from the others. This means that they eat very fast and are unable to relax when eating, as they are constantly worried that someone may try to get their share.

Using three or more bowls each with a tiny amount of food in means that he cannot guard all of them at once, and, of course, if he thinks there is more food than he needs he will be more inclined to invite you over to take a look. This does not, however, mean feeding the dog more, though the perception will be that there is plenty as there are a number of bowls scattered around the kitchen. Whilst he is eating from one, approach another and add something tasty, maybe a bit of grated cheese, some leftover vegetables, or some gravy. That way, you going to a bowl will predict better things so why would he want to keep you away?

With all aggression problems, however, it is advisable to seek expert help at the beginning of any programme to ensure that you get it right.

Barking

Barking when left alone in the house is a major problem for the owner as it inevitably affects the neighbours and causes friction. There is nothing more annoying than a dog next door who barks continuously when left.

When you first get your new puppy it may be the case that you have been very careful not to leave it on its own, you may even have taken a week off work to settle him in. The day then dawns when you must leave him with a nice new toy. But how stressful will it be when you go off and close the door on him?

If your puppy sleeps downstairs he is, of course, left for seven or eight hours on his own anyway, so why should it be a big deal to leave him during the day for a short time?

By far the best way is to start from day one and ensure that he is left every day in another room with the door closed, starting with a few minutes and building up to about half an hour. By waiting until he is asleep and then going into another room he will wake up and realize he is on his own. If he makes a huge fuss you will have to wait until he is quiet, and has remained quiet for at least two minutes before going back to him. If you can hear him moving around quietly then go in and make a fuss of him for the quiet behaviour. Increase the amount of time he is left slowly and don't always go to the same place, or he will get used to the idea that you are only upstairs because he can hear you moving around. Sometimes go out into the garden or drive the car around the block. In this way the puppy is given confidence that you will soon be back and there is nothing to worry about.

Also, try not to make it obvious to him that you are off out without him. Of course, there are lots of things that we do before going out that the puppy will pick up on. We shut windows, lock the door, put on our coat and outdoor shoes, turn off the television and pick up the car keys. He will soon learn that if this little ritual does not also include picking up his lead then he is in for a boring afternoon. We can make this far worse by adding a few clues which definitely tell him that he will be 'home alone'. Making a fuss of him and telling him we won't be long. Giving him toys and chews in his bed. Leaving on the radio, when we never usually have it on at all during the day. If we are worried about leaving him, he will automatically think that this is a bad thing. Don't treat him any differently prior to going out, don't make a fuss and say 'goodbye' and how much you will miss him. If you want to leave him a nice chew don't present it to him with an apology for going out, but hide it somewhere where he is most likely to find it. By building up the period he is left for slowly he won't become anxious when you go out and bark or chew. It might also be a good idea to warn the neighbours of the arrival of a new puppy and if you have to go out for any length of time ask them to pop in and let him out for you.

Barking at the door could be considered acceptable if the caller is a stranger, however most dogs will bark at any knock at the door and are not easily dissuaded from it once the door is opened.

This behaviour is learnt at a very early age as a knock on the door always predicts that someone will get up and go to the door and visitors come in. Of course, in the early days the puppy is the centre of attention, and he truly believes that all visitors have come especially to see him. This causes great excitement and leads to barking. We try to stop him by holding onto his collar and saying 'no' very loudly. This increases his efforts as he is frustrated by being restrained and he thinks that you are now joining in.

If in the early days we prevent the puppy from rushing to the door when visitors arrive and only allow him to say hello when he is calm he will not develop this annoying habit. The key to barking behaviour is usually the door bell or knocker as this indicates a stranger. We never knock at our own door and therefore the dog does not bark when we come in. Sometimes knock at the door yourself before coming and then ignore the dog when you enter the house until he calms down.

Teach the dog a different reaction to the door bell by having someone who has a key ring the bell and wait for two minutes before coming in. Give him a biscuit in his bed without going to the door so that the door bell indicates that he should wait in his bed for a reward.

Digging

Many dogs like to dig, this is a natural canine behaviour. Some breeds are better at this than others, terriers especially excel at digging. They will also dig for somewhere cool to lie in hot weather. This has carried over into our domestic dogs that seem to dig just for recreation.

We tend to reward digging behaviour with the very exciting game of chasing our dog around the garden, or by taking out a toy to take his mind off the lawn. This, of course, will result in your dog digging to get your attention. Call him immediately he begins to dig and redirect him to somewhere that he can dig, praise when he digs in the place that you want him to.

Of course, they also watch us digging and will sit and observe you digging and burying bulbs or plants and are just waiting for an opportunity to get in there and find out what is so special that you need to bury it. When they dig it up we then reinforce that idea by chasing them around the garden to get the prized shrub back. It is probably better not to let them watch, or to keep them out of the garden until the next day when they may have had the digging idea replaced with dreams of next-door's cat.

If your dog is a committed digger and gets huge pleasure from the act of digging it may be as well to designate a small piece of garden to him. Rather than trying to stop him digging at all, bury a few dog biscuits in a freshly dug plot and when you catch him digging in your rose beds show him that there is nothing of value there, but you will show him where the real treasure is buried. If you really do not want him to dig on any part of your garden then you can always buy him a child's sandpit and a couple of bags of builders' sand for him to dig in. If you do this then make sure you cover it up at night so the local cats don't use it as a toilet.

Inappropriate play

We all want our puppy to be friendly with other dogs and to have doggy friends who he can socialize with. It is not much fun, however, when out with your new puppy if a huge adult dog comes bounding across the park, completely out of control, followed by an owner yelling 'He only wants to play'. Your young puppy will, of course, be frightened to death. By allowing your young dog to play out-of-control games with other dogs he will grow up to believe that every dog he sees will want to play with him, and that playing involves biting at necks and ears, chasing round madly, holding the other dog on the ground and generally bullying him.

When playing with another dog they should be provided with toys and encouraged to play games that involve chasing each other for the toy or tugging games. That way if the other dog in the park does not have a toy it will not be of much interest.

If you own two dogs and they spend all their time playing rough games with each other then you are unlikely to be able to control their behaviour when out. Ensure that you are in control of the games and that they play much more with you than with other dogs. Should the older dog correct your puppy for biting too hard or just being a pest, back him up – the puppy needs to learn that this is not the way to treat older dogs and that you will not condone such behaviour. It is far better that your puppy plays with an older dog who is prepared to play games in moderation, but will tell the youngster when he has gone too far.

Attention-seeking behaviour

As with children, attention-seeking behaviour is best ignored. The trouble with this theory is that attention-seeking puppies are so cute.

Of course, not all attention-seeking activity becomes a problem, and the extent to which this occurs heavily depends on the reward the puppy gets for it. Rewards should not only be thought of as things he can eat or things he can play with. Talking to your puppy is a reward as is stroking him, scratching his ears or tummy. Even looking at him when he has diverted your attention from your favourite television programme can be considered a reward.

Attention-seeking behaviours can be such things as barking, chewing, paw licking, tail chasing, etc. A very common behaviour problem is barking when the owner is on the telephone. This almost always gets results as it is very difficult to hold a conversation when the dog is barking and will inevitably mean that the owner has to break off the conversation if only to tell the dog to be quiet, thereby rewarding the behaviour by paying attention to it.

How then can you deal with the behaviour by ignoring it? Do not start by waiting for a real telephone call, but set up the situation. Dial your own number from your mobile and answer it. You can then hang up the mobile so as not to run up your phone bill. Pretend to be holding a conversation and as soon as your dog makes a noise slam down the receiver with an annoyed expression and stamp out of the room. This is just what he didn't want; remember he is after attention not isolation. If you have a real call during this period of re-education then put the dog in another room before answering the telephone.

Chewing as an attention getter works well when your puppy is bored and wants a game. Having tried to get you to play by bringing you his toys and not getting the attention he wants, he may well play for a while on his own. When bored with the game his teeth may inadvertently stray onto the leg of the coffee table, you will immediately jump up saying 'no! no!' and give him an alternative for his chewing activity. Now you are paying attention to the toy he wanted you to play with in the first place. He will soon learn to go straight for those items he is not meant to have, such as the TV remote, glasses case, furniture. In the case of the TV remote and such items he will be able to instigate huge games by chasing round the house with them in his mouth and getting you to chase him.

If you pay attention to the type of behaviours you do want and reward him when he is lying quietly by offering a game, or giving a food treat, this type of behaviour will be uppermost in his mind when he wants to gain attention. When you first introduce your puppy to the lounge, where he possibly has not been allowed until his house-training is over, take him in on a lead after he has had exercise, and encourage him to be calm and quiet. He will soon learn that if he wishes to have your company in the evenings this is the way to earn that privilege.

When your puppy pinches items that he is not supposed to have don't be tempted to chase after him, thereby showing him that this item is of great value to you and you are prepared to indulge him in endless games of chase to regain possession. The best strategy is to walk quietly past him and carelessly drop a food treat, when he leaves the article do not grab it up and hide it or you will reinforce his belief that this is a highly-prized possession that you are keen to keep for yourself. Ignore the discarded item and drop another treat a bit further away. Once the puppy has his mind on other things quietly pick up the object of his attention when he is not looking and place it out of his reach. By showing no interest in it yourself he will no longer be fixated on it as a means of gaining your attention. If he then picks up a dog toy pay great attention to that and offer to play with him. He will then be more inclined to pick up those items which he is allowed to have as a way of making you take notice of him.

Tail chasing and paw licking are also behaviours which can elicit a lot of attention for different reasons. Tail chasing is of course funny and puppies can gain everyone's attention with a bit of silly behaviour. You can turn this one into a trick by putting one cue such as 'spin' whenever he does it and reward it. You should then only reward if you have asked him to do it.

Paw licking/nibbling usually results from the puppy having grass seeds in his paws or maybe a skin irritation. When this first manifests itself it is best to pop your puppy into the vet to ensure that there is nothing sinister brewing. He will probably give some form of medication. To ensure that you are not constantly trying to verbally and physically prevent your puppy from licking, thereby reinforcing the behaviour, get an Elizabethan collar to prevent your puppy from doing it. If you pop this on every time he starts licking he will soon stop, as he will not want to have the collar on.

Worktop surfers

There are occasions when gentle environmental correction is useful and a worktop surfer is one!

All dogs will try to find free food when they can, very young dogs are often hungry, and the smell of food being prepared on the work surface is too hard to resist! The problem is usually at its peak at around 5–6 months of age, as the young dog grows tall enough to reach the counter. Crumbs and scraps falling on the floor further reinforce the behaviour. You may find yourself constantly telling your dog to 'get down'. This approach will not improve matters as you are only interrupting the behaviour and not actually teaching your dog not to put his feet on the counter!

Try the following, it may help. Buy a reel of brown parcel tape and place long lengths of it along the top edge of your worktop turning the ends under to stick it to the surface. You will need to replace the tape on a daily basis or more often if it becomes untidy. It will be a nuisance to you but it is only for a limited time and well worth the effort if it works. When your dog puts his paws on the worktop he should find the feel of the sticky tape unpleasant, you will not need to say anything to your dog, he has to learn that it is what he does (putting paws on the counter) that causes the unpleasant feeling. In other words it is the environment that is correcting your dog and not you, the correction should in no way be associated with you. This may take several days or a week or two for the behaviour to cease. Even when you think your dog has stopped the behaviour keep the tape in place for a few weeks in case your dog is tempted by some really tasty smell. Keeping worktops free of food when you are not around will also help.

A warning! Some owners are advised to use noisy apparatus such as pebbles in cans or baking trays or even water squirting bottles to stop unwanted behaviour. Although they may seem harmless at the time many dogs can be traumatized by their use and your relationship with your dog may be damaged. It is very difficult to recover a dog from trauma. Please seek professional help and even then question the methods: are they suitable for *your* dog?

12

the older dog

In this chapter you will learn:
- how to care for an older dog
- how to look for the signs of ageing
- how to exercise as appropriate for your dog's age.

Different breeds tend to age at different rates. As a generalization the bigger the dog the earlier the onset of old age. With some slight adjustments to their lifestyle most dogs are able to stay active and fit during their later years. Signs of old age are graying around the muzzle, an increase or decrease in weight, sleeping longer and deeper, tooth decay, thinning coat, maybe becoming more intolerant of other pets or being groomed.

Feeding

Because the older dog may take less exercise their total energy requirement may be less.

- Use good quality food. Foods of high energy and nutrient density mean your dog can eat smaller meals and still obtain the essential nutrients.
- It is a good idea to divide the daily food intake into several small, highly digestible meals.
- Ensure that the diet you use is a balanced one with the correct vitamin and mineral content.

Exercise

The older dog still enjoys and requires regular exercise.

- Rather than one long strenuous walk, take your dog for two or three shorter walks.
- For short-haired dogs supply a coat to keep them warm.
- If your dog enjoys swimming make sure he is dried thoroughly afterwards, and do not allow him to swim if the weather is particularly cold.
- When throwing a toy or ball for your dog do not throw it too high, as your dog will often twist as he jumps and could injure muscles or ligaments.
- When the weather is hot make sure that your dog does not get over heated or dehydrated.

Training

Keeping the brain active helps delay signs of dementia. Despite the saying, many older dogs are capable of learning new tricks, or perhaps improving on old ones.

Teach your dog to:

- Retrieve
- Give a paw
- Touch a target
- Stay or wait
- Sit
- Lie down
- Improve his recall or lead walking.

Health

Just like humans as they get older dogs can be affected by ill health. Always err on the side of caution and if your dog seems unwell visit your veterinary surgeon.

Here are a few ailments to watch for:

- Stiffness of joints
- Bad eyesight (cataracts)
- Bad breath
- Lumps or growths
- Deafness
- Confusion
- Excessive drinking. This may be the onset of diabetes.

With regular veterinary checks, good diet and a knowledgeable owner many dogs live long and happy lives.

13 recipes for your dog

In this chapter you will learn:
- how to cook the best training treats
- how to cook your own dog biscuits.

Shop bought treats can be high in sugar, chemicals and preservatives, too many can have a detrimental effect and also put weight on your dog. Also, shop bought treats can be rather bland and when competeing with the environment, training something like a recall calls for special reinforcements. Below are some home-made treats that your dogs will love.

Chessy chomps

2 cups wholemeal flour
1 heaped dessert spoon garlic powder
1 tbsp brewers yeast
1 cup grated cheese
1 egg
1 cup water

Mix the flour, garlic and brewers yeast together, then stir in other ingredients. Knead the dough well, then roll out to ¼ inch thickness. Using a pastry cutter or knife cut into biscuit shapes and place on a greased baking tray. Bake for 30 minutes at 150°C/gas mark 2 or until lightly browned. Store in an airtight box or tin.

Liver cake

1 lb liver
1 beaten egg
½ lb flour

Liquidize the liver. Add the flour and beaten egg. Cook on a medium heat until the middle is firm. Leave to cool in the tin. Keep some in a sealed container in the fridge for immediate use and freeze the rest as it does not keep well. As a variation add a chopped clove of garlic.

Home-made dog biscuits

8 oz sausage meat
2–3 fl oz stock or water
8 oz plain wholemeal flour

Preheat oven to 180°C/350°F/gas mark 4. Mix the sausage meat and flour with the stock to form a stiff dough. Roll out on a floured surface to ½ inch thickness, cut into squares, or roll into mini sausages. Place on *ungreased* baking sheets and bake for 30–50 minutes depending on their size. Take care not to burn, but they need to be hard. Cool before serving.

Dog biscuits

1 lb wholemeal flour
1 egg
3 oz melted lard
1 Oxo cube
$^{1}/_{2}$ pint milk, or milk/water mixture
$^{1}/_{2}$ lb cooked ox liver

Mince the liver. Mix all the ingredients together and add the liquid. Roll out to just over $^{1}/_{4}$ inch thick. Cut out with a 2 inch cutter or into squares. Bake at 100°C in a slow oven for about 2 hours until crisp.

Dog biscuits

3 oz wholemeal flour
$^{1}/_{2}$ oz fat or dripping
$1^{1}/_{2}$ pints milk
2–3 fl oz stock or water
2 tbsp grated cheese
3 Oxo cubes

Rub the fat into the flour. Add the well-crumbled Oxo cubes and grated cheese. Mix with milk (or milk mixture) into a stiff dough. Roll out $^{1}/_{4}$ inch thick and cut into squares. Put on a floured baking sheet and bake in moderately hot oven (180°C) for 45 minutes. When cold, store in an airtight tin.

Liver treats

1 lb liver
1 clove garlic

Bring the garlic and liver to boil in a little water, simmer for five minutes until cooked through. Drain on kitchen paper and cut into small pieces. Spread on a baking sheet and bake at about 150°C for about half an hour. Turn off oven and leave until cold. This doesn't keep very well so freeze what you are not going to use immediately.

Tuna training treats

2 6oz cans of tuna in water – do not drain

2 eggs

1–1½ cups wholemeal flour

1 tbsp garlic powder

Mash the tuna and water in a bowl with a fork and then liquefy in a blender or food processor. Add extra drops of water if needed to liquefy completely. Pour into a bowl and add the flour and garlic powder. The consistency should be like a cake mix. Spread on a greased baking tray. Bake at 180°C for 15 minutes. Use a pizza cutter and cut into tiny squares. This recipe freezes well.

taking it further

Useful organizations

Association of Pet Behaviour Counsellors
PO Box 46
Worcester
WR8 9YS
Tel: 01386 751151
www.apbc.co.uk

Association of Pet Dog Trainers
PO Box 17
Kempsford
GL7 4WZ
Tel: 01285 810811
www.apdt.co.uk

The Blue Cross
Shilton Road
Burford
Oxfordshire
OX18 4PF
Tel: 01993 822651
www.bluecross.org.uk

The Dogs Home Battersea
4 Battersea Park Road
London
SW8 2AA
Tel: 0171 622 3626
www.dogshome.org

The Dogs Trust
17 Wakley Street
London
EC1V 7LT
Tel: 0171 837 0006
www.dogstrust.org.uk

The Kennel Club
1–5 Clarges Street
Piccadilly
London
W1A 8AB
Tel: 0171 493 6651/629 5828
www.the-kennel-club.org.uk

Royal Veterinary College
Camden Campus
Royal College Street
London
NW1 0TU
Tel: 0171 468 5000

RSPCA
Causeway
Horsham
West Sussex
RH12 1HG
Tel: 01403 264181
www.rspca.org.uk

Recommended reading

Burch & Bailey (1998) *How Dogs Learn*, Howell Book House Inc.

Donaldson, J. (1996) *The Culture Clash*, James and Kenneth Publishers.

Eaton, B. (2002) *Dominance: Fact or Fiction*, Barry Eaton.

Mackinnon, S. (2004) *A Guide to Effective Food Use in Training*.

McConnell, P. (2003) *Other End of the Leash*, Random House Inc.

Parry, P. (2005) *Patsy Parry's Puppy Problems! The good, the bad and the downright ugly*, Crosskeys Select.

Pryor, K. (2002) *Don't Shoot the Dog*, Ringpress Books.

Ruggas, T. (1997) *On talking terms with dogs: Calming Signals*, Legacy By Mail Inc.

Whitehead, S. (1999) *Hands Off!*, Alpha.

Whitehead, S. (2003) *Puppy Training for Kids*, Kenilworth Press Ltd.

Whitehead, S. (2004) *The Puppy Survival Guide*, Alpha.

Woodcock, D. (2002) *Preventing Puppy Problems*, DogSense Publications.

All books available through Crosskeys Books at www.crosskeysbooks.co.uk

Accredited courses

Association of Pet Dog Trainers
PO Box 17
Kempsford
GL7 4WZ

Animal Care College
Ascot House
High Street
Ascot
Berkshire
SL5 7JG
Tel: 0870 730 8433
www.corsini.co.uk

COAPE
PO Box 6
Fortrose
Ross-shire
IV10 8WB
Tel: 0800 783 0817
www.coape.co.uk